Study Strategies Made Easy

by
Leslie Davis, M.Ed. and Sandi Sirotowitz, M.Ed.
with Harvey C. Parker, Ph.D.

Illustrated by Richard Dimatteo

Specialty Press, Inc.
Plantation, Florida
(800) 233-9273

DEDICATION

To Alisa, Brent and Kevin - our helpers, critics and inspirations!

Illustrated by Richard Dimatteo

Specialty Press, Inc.
300 Northwest 70th Avenue, Suite 102
Plantation, Florida 33317
(954) 792-8100 • (800) 233-9273.

Printed in the United States of America

ISBN 1-886941-03-3

Library of Congress Cataloging-in-Publication Data

Davis, Leslie
      Study strategies made easy : a practical plan for school success : organization, learning style, communication, reading comprehension, note taking, memorization, test taking, homework, stress management / by Leslie Davis and Sandi Sirotowitz with Harvey C. Parker
           p.   cm.
      ISBN 1-886941-03-3
      1. Study skills -- Handbooks, manuals, etc.   I. Sirotowitz, Sandi,
          II. Parker, Harvey C.   III. Title.
LB1049.D39   1996
371.3'028' 12--dc20   96-26195
                                                                    CIP

ACKNOWLEDGMENTS

Since opening our educational center in 1978, we have taught thousands of students how to become successful learners. In those years we observed and listened to the concerns, frustrations, and fears of our students, their parents and their teachers about students' in-school progress. It all seemed to boil down into one fact: capable students with involved and well-meaning parents and teachers were missing one important ingredient for achievement. They did not know how to acquire, retain, and recall the wealth of facts necessary for them to do well without stress. As we taught strategies to achieve study efficiency, parents and teachers kept asking if we could "put it together" so schools and students could have what we taught. So, we did. However, we never expected that what began as an in-house program for our own center would take so many years of our working lives in the myriad of revisions. We also never expected to receive the wonderful encouragement and support from so many people. To all of you, thank you.

To Marvin Sirotowitz, without whose patient insistence that we learn to use computers this project would still be in its infancy. To Lynn Davis for his always rational, rock-solid support. Thank you both for always being there.

To our editor, Harvey Parker, Ph.D., who cares so much about children and recognizing their needs intuitively knew what we wanted to say and could say it better.

To our incredibly professional staff at Educational & Diagnostic Services, whose field testing and invaluable input during these past eighteen years helped to refine and enhance the final program. With special thanks to Maddy Levitt.

To our students at E.D.S. who constantly and joyfully prove our philosophy that all students can succeed and even enjoy the process of learning once they are given the tools. A special thanks to Josh Baimel, Desha Beder and Chris Calvert.

To Brent Davis, who typed the first edition and actually learned the strategies through osmosis.

To Alisa Cowan, who has the talent to turn even prosaic topics into interesting prose, and did.

To our very special colleagues and friends from the Association of Independent Learning Centers. How can we ever thank such a professional group of true educators who inspired and motivated us.

To Geri Backer, our right hand at E.D.S., who put up with the insanity and kept things running so smoothly.

TABLE OF CONTENTS

INSTRUCTIONS

A NOTE TO STUDENTS

This book is written just for you! If you've ever wondered how good students learn so easily and do so well, this program will take that mystery out of the learning process. If you follow the strategies in this book, you will be able to take control of and responsibility for your own learning.

First, take the inventory of your present study skills. This will give you an idea of your current study habits. Then, proceed through the chapters, paying special attention to those areas of need that you identified through the inventory. Do not skip any strategy, even if it was not an area of particular need for you. You may discover a new and more efficient strategy that will help you improve what you are already doing fairly well.

Study Strategies Made Easy is divided into the following skill areas:

1. **Organizational Strategies** will teach you steps to organize your study time, materials, and environment.

2. **Learning Style Strategies** will help you become more familiar with how you learn best.

3. **Communication Strategies** will provide you with tools to become more effective in communicating your specific needs to teachers.

4. **Reading Comprehension Strategies** will teach you how to identify and understand the main points that teachers and textbook publishers think are important and therefore include on their tests.

5. **Note-Taking Strategies** will show you various ways to take and organize your notes so that you can turn them into useful study sheets.

6. **Memorization Strategies** will provide you with ways to learn material and use ten memorization techniques that are tailored to your own learning style.

7. **Test Taking Strategies** breaks down the different types of tests including those dreaded mid-term and final exams, and offers suggestions for succeeding on all of them.

8. **Homework Strategies** focus on developing productive habits for completing homework assignments.

9. **Stress Management Strategies** will help you handle stress from school and become a more positive thinker.

As you learn a new strategy, immediately put it into practice on your own school work. Remember that the more you practice, the more natural a strategy will become for you and the easier learning will become. We hope that you not only learn new and better ways to achieve your goals, but that you begin to have fun as you learn!

INSTRUCTIONS

A NOTE TO PARENTS

Why are you considering this book? Because you want your child to be successful in school. You are sure that your child has the basic academic skills – but you also wonder if he needs more. You wonder, has my child been taught the most important skill – how to learn? Just as your child had to be taught the skills of reading, math, and writing, he must also be taught the skills for efficient and effective studying.

Is your child struggling just to pass his subjects? Or is your child a good student taking challenging subjects and working too many hours to maintain top grades? For both of these students the answer to easing stress and improving grades is to learn how to learn – efficiently.

The best gift you can give your children is the gift of learning the tools to help them become independent, efficient, motivated, and ultimately successful throughout their school careers. The best gift that you can give your child is in your hands right now – *Study Strategies Made Easy*

To assist you in this process please refer to the section entitled "Lesson Plans for Instructors" in Appendix C. Here you will find our suggestions for presenting many of the strategies discussed in the program. This section along with the Answer Key found in Appendix A are perforated and can be removed.

A NOTE TO INSTRUCTORS

Teachers know that if we tell a child what to think, we make him a slave to our knowledge. But, if we teach a child how to think, we make all knowledge his slave. That philosophy guided us as we wrote *Study Strategies Made Easy*.

Study Strategies Made Easy is being successfully taught to students in grades six through twelve. We want to form a partnership with you to demystify the learning process for your students. You know these students. They are the ones in your classes who:
- are disorganized,
- can't get work completed or turned in,
- don't appear to understand what you expect of them,
- cannot pick out important points from your lectures or their text books,
- either cannot take notes or if they can, don't seem to use them,
- are not successful on your tests.

They are also your students who work too hard, stress too much, and try to burn the candle at both ends. If you feel that your students need more efficient and effective ways to achieve in your classes, begin teaching *Study Strategies Made Easy* and give your students a gift of learning.

To assist you in this process please refer to the section entitled "Lesson Plans for Instructors" in Appendix C. Here you will find our suggestions for presenting many of the strategies discussed in the program. This section along with the Answer Key found in Appendix A are perforated and can be removed.

BEFORE WE BEGIN . . .
A CHECKLIST OF STUDY STRATEGIES

Before you begin *Study Strategies Made Easy*, take a few minutes to evaluate your present study skills. Answer the questions below to evaluate your study strengths and weaknesses. Read each question. If you *almost* always do what is asked, write "Yes"; *almost never* do what is asked, write "No"; *sometimes* do what is asked, write "S". Then, write the number of your **yes** answers in the score box on the next page. How are *your* present study skills rated?

ORGANIZATION

_____ 1. Do I have all of the supplies I need for school?

_____ 2. Do I keep my notebooks and materials organized so that I can easily find what I need?

_____ 3. Do I keep a schedule of study times and activities?

_____ 4. Do I write my assignments in an assignment notebook?

_____ 5. Do I have an organized plan for the order I do my assignments?

_____ 6. Do I complete and turn in my assignments on time?

_____ 7. Do I keep track of my grades on a weekly basis?

_____ 8. Do I keep and follow a written plan to complete long-term assignments?

LEARNING STYLE

_____ 9. Do I use my best style of learning when I study?

_____ 10. Do I understand where, when, and how I study best?

COMMUNICATION

_____ 11. Do my teachers usually see my behavior in the classroom in a positive way?

_____ 12. Do I usually know what each teacher expects of me?

_____ 13. Do I effectively talk to my teachers when I need help?

_____ 14. Do I discuss school-related problems I might have with my teachers?

_____ 15. Do I communicate well with other students and show respect for them?

READING COMPREHENSION

_____ 16. Can I identify topics, main ideas, and supporting details in a reading selection?

_____ 17. Do I understand without having to reread, what I am reading in my textbooks?

_____ 18. Can I summarize what I read in my own words?

_____ 19. Do I use signal words to help me identify important information in my textbooks?

_____ 20. Do I preview the textbook chapters?

_____ 21. Do I consistently read my textbook?

_____ 22. Do I have a successful method to learn new vocabulary and remember it during and after a test?

NOTE-TAKING

_____ 23. Do I take notes from lectures?

_____ 24. Do I get the important points from my teachers' lectures?

_____ 25. Do I use different ways to take accurate notes?

_____ 26. Do I use abbreviations for note-taking?

_____ 27. Do I turn my notes into study sheets?

_____ 28. Do I combine information from the textbook with my lecture notes?

_____ 29. Do I review my notes over a period of time?

MEMORIZATION

_____ 30. Do I know different ways to memorize beside reading information over and over?

_____ 31. Do I use different ways to memorize information?

_____ 32. When I take tests, do I remember most of the facts I tried to memorize?

TEST-TAKING

_____ 33. While taking a test, do I very carefully follow directions?

_____ 34. Do I use appropriate strategies for taking different kinds of tests?

_____ 35. Do I keep old tests to use at a later time?

_____ 36. Do I analyze my errors from old tests to determine a pattern?

_____ 37. Do I effectively prepare for mid-terms and final exams?

_____ 38. Am I satisfied with my study habits?

_____ 39. Am I pleased with my grades?

DOING HOMEWORK

_____ 40. Do I use an assignment book?

_____ 41. Do I do homework in an environment that allows me to concentrate?

_____ 42. Do I spend enough time on homework to do a thorough job?

_____ 43. Do I complete homework by the time it is due?

STRESS MANAGEMENT

_____ 44. Am I confident that I can do well in school?

_____ 45. Do I have a positive, optimistic outlook about my schoolwork?

_____ 46. Do I feel as relaxed as most other students do about schoolwork and tests?

_____ 47. Do I know strategies to help me reduce stress and relax?

HIGHLIGHT YOUR RATING:		
42-47	YES = Superior Study Habits	SCORE: _____
36-41	YES = Good Study Habits	
29-35	YES = Average Study Habits	
below 28	YES = Needs Improvement	

Look over each of your responses and analyze your study strategy strengths and weaknesses. Your "Yes" responses indicate study strategies you are already using that are working well for you. If you answered with more "No" responses under one heading then as you progress through the *Study Strategies Made Easy* program you will learn to improve your study habits.

CHAPTER 1
ORGANIZATIONAL STRATEGIES

Some people are just naturally organized while others have to learn organization. If you are lucky enough to be a person who always knows where everything you own is, who rarely misplaces things or misses an appointment or a deadline, you probably won't need to do much work getting yourself organized. But, if you are like most of us, you can probably use a little organization refresher course.

We started this workbook with organization because it is extremely important to be organized if you want to succeed in school or in just about anything. If you think of it, there are probably a lot of things you need to keep track of to stay organized: your money, lunch, clothes, CDs, etc. However, to be successful in school the most important things to keep track of are your school supplies (books, paper, notebooks, homework, etc.), your time, your grades, and your assignments.

Organization is a pretty broad skill, and like all the other skills discussed in this workbook, we have broken it down into strategies. There are seven organizational strategies presented in this section.

- **Organizing Your School Supplies**
- **Organizing Your Study Area**
- **Organizing Your Time**
- **Organizing Your Assignments**
- **Prioritizing Your Work**
- **Organizing Your Grades**
- **Organizing Your Long-Term Research Projects**

Strategy
Organizing Your School Supplies

Directions: Here is a handy "shopping list" of school supplies. Check the supplies that you need and take the shopping list with you to the store to make your purchases.

SCHOOL SUPPLIES SHOPPING LIST

NOTEBOOKS, etc.
- ❑ one three-ring notebook (2" or 3" rings) for all subjects
- ❑ one three-ring notebook (1/2" rings) for each subject
- ❑ spiral notebooks, one per class
- ❑ dividers with pockets, a different color for each class
- ❑ a case for highlighters, pens, pencils, etc.

ASSIGNMENT BOOKS, etc.
to write daily and long-term assignments
- ❑ a teacher or student planning book
- ❑ a calendar type book (also called appointment book)
- ❑ a calendar with large empty spaces
- ❑ electronic schedule and assignment keeper

IMPORTANT BOOKS, etc.
- ❑ a dictionary
- ❑ a thesaurus
- ❑ an up-to-date atlas
- ❑ access to an encyclopedia
- ❑ a library card

FILES
- ❑ a 3 X 5 or larger filebox and ruled index cards

Three suggested methods for keeping old tests and homework:
- ❑ 1. a three-ring notebook divided for each class
- ❑ 2. an accordion file folder with enough pockets for each class
- ❑ 3. a crate to hold file folders for each class

OTHER NECESSARY STUFF
- ❑ pens, pencils, colored pencils, crayons, and erasers
- ❑ a pencil sharpener
- ❑ a ruler
- ❑ markers
- ❑ highlighters (yellow and at least one other color)
- ❑ glue, rubber cement, tape
- ❑ scissors
- ❑ stapler and staples
- ❑ hole punch
- ❑ paper clips
- ❑ rubber bands
- ❑ reinforcers for notebook paper

Exercise

Organizing Your School Supplies

If you've bought your materials, your next step is to organize them and keep them organized. Truly, it's so much easier to reach into a bookbag and pull out the paper you're looking for instead of a half-eaten doughnut turned to stone. It also will save you energy to keep a notebook or folders that are labeled with contents that actually coincide with the labels. Since our philosophy is to "do the worst first," we'll begin with your BOOKBAG. Dump yours out now.

A. **Look at the contents of your bookbag and answer these questions by checking "Y" for Yes and "N" for No.**

Y   N

___ ___ 1. Is there anything moving? *If yes, call the local humane society.*

___ ___ 2. Are there papers that have been missing for months and you thought were lost forever? *If yes, file them where you can find them.*

___ ___ 3. Are there papers you no longer need to carry to and from school? *If yes: for any important papers, decide where they need to go, and file any old tests or notes. For anything else that you haven't seen, don't need and never will, TRASH IT.*

___ ___ 4. Are scissors, pens, highlighters and other tools thrown in everywhere? *If yes, put them in a separate case that is easy to use and easy to find.*

B. **Notebooks or folders are actually useful for storing papers and notes. So take your notebooks and folders out now and look through them.**

Y   N

___ ___ 1. Are there books and folders without labels or dividers, and are they so alike that you cannot tell science from English? *If yes, get a different colored folder for each class. If you use a three-ring binder, get dividers, one for each class, and keep papers in their proper sections.*

___ ___ 2. Are notes from social studies, science, English, math and Spanish in one notebook in no particular order? *If yes, and after you have your dividers, put notes in the sections you've labeled for them.*

C. **Choose one day every week to clean out your bookbag and go through your notebooks. Reorganize anything that's not in order.**

Strategy

Organizing Your Study Area

Why organize your study area? If you always keep your school work and materials in the same place, you will be able to find them quickly. No more lost papers or lost time searching for them. Your energy will be spent on doing great work.

Suggestions:

FIND A PLACE TO STUDY

1. An area that is well-lit and free from distractions.
2. A table or desk and a comfortable chair.

FIND A PLACE TO STORE SCHOOL MATERIALS

1. In your study area, find a place to store your school materials:
   a. some shelves in a closet and/or some drawers in a desk.
   b. plastic crates.
2. If you still forget materials you need in school, try this:
   a. as soon as you complete your work, put your work and books in your book bag.
   b. place the book bag in a crate that is right by the door from which you leave for school.   This will prevent morning rush and forgotten papers.

Directions:

Use the space below to list improvements you can make to have a better study environment and area for materials.

_____

_____

_____

_____

_____

_____

Strategy
Organizing Your Time

This strategy will help you to evaluate whether you are budgeting your time as efficiently as you might. If not, it will be easy for you to rearrange your time to get more done and have more fun.

Directions: **Refer to the sample schedule below and fill out the schedule sheet on the following page.**

1. Write your daily after-school activities for the week. Include such things as music lessons, sports, and anything else you do weekly. Monday and Tuesday are filled out in the sample schedule sheet.
2. Draw a box around the remaining empty time spaces. These will be the hours you have free to do school work and study. In our sample, some are already filled out while others are blank.
3. For each day, add the number of hours that are free for school work and study and write the amounts in the space marked "available times" at the bottom. Look at the empty boxes in the sample to show how your schedule will look before you fill them in with activities.
4. For one week, note how long you spend each day on homework or studying. Write the subject and the amount of time you studied or worked on each subject in each day's space. Add the number of these hours and write that amount in the space marked "Time Used for Study" at the bottom.

SAMPLE

WEEKLY SCHEDULE SHEET							week of Oct. 12
TIME	**MONDAY**	**TUESDAY**	**WEDNESDAY**	**THURSDAY**	**FRIDAY**	**SATURDAY**	**SUNDAY**
4:00 - 4:30		Journalism					
4:30 - 5:00		meeting					
5:00 - 5:30	Sci.						
5:30 - 6:00	Eng 15 min	⚓					
6:00 - 6:30	Span 15 min	⚓					
6:30 - 7:00	Dinner	Dinner	Dinner	Dinner	Dinner		
7:00 - 7:30	Babysitting						
7:30 - 8:00		Math					
8:00 - 8:30		Soc. Studies					
8:30 - 9:00		Eng.					
9:00 - 9:30		Sci.					
9:30 - 10:00							
10:00 - 10:30							
AVAILABLE TIME	3 1/2 hrs	2 1/2 hrs	4 hrs	4 hrs	1 1/2 hrs		2 hrs
TIME USED FOR STUDY	1 hr	2 hrs					

WEEKLY SCHEDULE SHEET

TIME	MONDAY	TUESDAY	WEDNESDAY	THURSDAY	FRIDAY	SATURDAY	SUNDAY
4:00 - 4:30 or earlier							
5:00 - 5:30							
5:30 - 6:00							
6:00 - 6:30							
6:30 - 7:00							
7:00 - 7:30							
7:30 - 8:00							
8:00 - 8:30							
8:30 - 9:00							
9:00 - 9:30							
9:30 - 10:00							
10:00 - 10:30 or after							
AVAILABLE TIME / TIME USED FOR STUDY							

8

Exercise
Evaluating How You
Organized Your Time

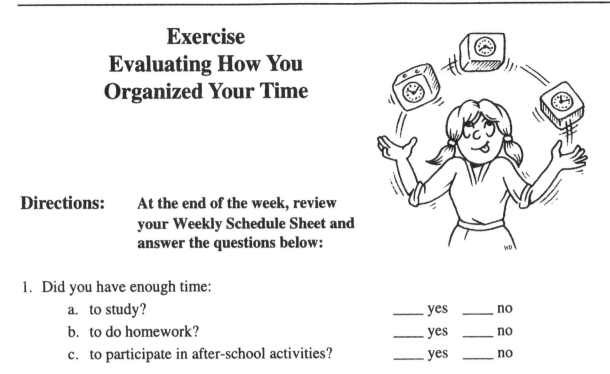

Directions: At the end of the week, review your Weekly Schedule Sheet and answer the questions below:

1. Did you have enough time:
   a. to study?   _____ yes _____ no
   b. to do homework?   _____ yes _____ no
   c. to participate in after-school activities?   _____ yes _____ no

If you answered "yes" then you budgeted your time well. If, on the other hand, you answered "no" and felt rushed or that you couldn't do all you wanted to do, look again at the schedule you kept and adjust your schedule accordingly.

2. Can you make some changes to:
   a. add more time to study?   _____ yes _____ no
   b. spend less time watching T.V.?   _____ yes _____ no
   c. spend less time talking on the phone?   _____ yes _____ no
   d. rearrange your after-school work hours? _____ yes _____ no

3. Plan a more efficient schedule and write it in the Weekly Schedule Sheet on the next page. In Appendix B you will find an extra schedule sheet which you can copy for future use.

4. Use the schedule as a guide to help you increase your efficient use of your after-school hours.

5. Become a "time juggler." Successful people are often people who budget their time so efficiently that they become "time jugglers" and do more in one day than seems possible. Strive to become that person.

WEEKLY SCHEDULE SHEET

WEEK OF _____

TIME	MONDAY	TUESDAY	WEDNESDAY	THURSDAY	FRIDAY	SATURDAY	SUNDAY
4:00 - 5:00 or earlier							
5:00 - 5:30							
5:30 - 6:00							
6:00 - 6:30							
6:30 - 7:00							
7:00 - 7:30							
7:30 - 8:00							
8:00 - 8:30							
8:30 - 9:00							
9:00 - 9:30							
9:30 - 10:00							
10:00 - 10:30 or after							
AVAILABLE TIME / TIME USED FOR STUDY							

10

Strategy
Prioritizing Your Work

You have learned to organize your materials, your environment, and your time for work. Now learn how to organize the work itself by prioritizing.

Directions:

1. See the sample below as a guide to filling out the *Get It Done Today* list on page 12. First, in your assignment book, write every assignment given for every class every day. Then refer to the assignment book when you get home.

2. Write all assignments and study sessions on the *Get It Done Today* list.

3. Decide which assignments must be done immediately and which can be put off for a while. We suggest doing the worst first and making the easiest last as your reward.

4. Under "Priority," write "1" by the assignment you plan to do first, "2" by the one you will work on second, etc.

5. Check off each assignment on your to-do list as you complete it. You will get a sense of accomplishment when you see your to-do list dwindle. Finally, write any work not completed on the next day's to-do list. An extra *Get It Done Today* list can be found in Appendix B and can be copied for your future use.

GET IT DONE **TODAY**

Date __March 2__

Priority	Assignment	Date Due	Complete
3	Work on plant life report	3/10	☐
2	Math page 204 prob. 1-25	3/4	☑
1	Social studies quiz #New Deal	3/4	☑
3	Call Mike to go over poetry project	3/4	☐
4	Write recall questions--Sci. chapt. 7	3/7	☐
			☐

GET IT DONE TODAY

Date _____

Priority	Assignment	Date Due	Completed
_____	_____		☐
_____	_____		☐
_____	_____		☐
_____	_____		☐
_____	_____		☐
_____	_____		☐
_____	_____		☐
_____	_____		☐
_____	_____		☐
_____	_____		☐

Strategy
Organizing Your Grades

We all feel terrific when we earn good grades, so at the beginning of each grading period, target the grades that you want to achieve. This strategy will help you to keep track of your grades for each week of every quarter. When you keep accurate records you will take control over the grades you earn and get the grades you want.

Directions:

Final Test Scores

Refer to the sample grade chart below.

1. On the grade chart on the following page, write your name, circle the number of the current grading quarter and write its beginning date.

2. Write each of your courses in the left "course" column and the grade you want to receive for each course.

3. Write in **all** the grades you receive during each week. Use the grade key on the chart for the type of assignments.

4. Review weekly to make sure you are on the track you want.

5. An extra Grade Chart can be found in Appendix B for future use.

SAMPLE

GRADE CHART											

Quarter 1 ②3 4
Beginning date _Nov 11_____   Name:_Chris_____

KEY: T= test Q=quiz
HW=homework
P=project

COURSE / GRADE	WEEK # 1	2	3	4	5	6	7	8	9	REPORT CARD GRADES
English Grade I want A	Q 98 T 90	HW A T 100	P 102							
Bio Grade I want B	Lab 89 HW 92	T 72	Q 82							
Algebra Grade I want B	HW 92 Q 98	HW 98 T 77 P 90	HW 92 T 89							
World History Grade I want A	T90 HW 100	Q 88 HW 98	T 90							

GRADE CHART

Quarter 1 2 3 4
Beginning date _____

COURSE	WEEK 1	2	3	4	5	6	7	8	9	Report Card Grade
Grade I want_____										
Grade I want_____										
Grade I want_____										
Grade I want_____										
Grade I want_____										
Grade I want_____										
Grade I want_____										

Strategy

Organizing Your Long-Term Research Projects

When a term paper or research project isn't due for a long time, we tend to put it off until the last minute and then we PANIC! This strategy will help you to break large projects down into manageable steps. While it may be tempting to skip steps, if you follow the directions you will get your work done on time and without stress for you and your parents.

Directions:

1. Refer to the sample form on the following pages. The sample comes from an assignment given in a science class. The information in the box labeled "Requirements" is what the teacher has directed must be included. The "Pre-Write," "First Write," and "Home Stretch" are what you decide to include.

2. A blank Goal-Setting Form can be found in Appendix B for future use.

Strategy

Organizing Your Long-Term Research Projects by Setting Goals

Goal-Setting Form for a Long-Term Research Project

REQUIREMENTS:

Assignment: <u>The Environment and Ways to Improve It</u>

✔ written; # of pages or words: <u>7 pages</u>

_____ oral; amount of time _____

Format requirements: <u>double spaced, 1 inch margins, bibliography page, works cited page</u>

Other requirements: <u>No more than one printed encyclopedia plus one computer ency-clopedia, no less than 5 sources</u>

DATE DUE: <u>March 1</u>

TARGET GRADE: A

	Due by Date	Doing ✔ Done ✗

THE PRE-WRITE		

STEP 1: TENTATIVE TOPICS

If the teacher gives you a choice of topics, consider two that are of interest to you.

TENTATIVE TOPICS   <u>2/1</u>   <u>X</u>
1. <u>Pollution</u>
2. <u>The Oceans</u>

STEP 2: PRELIMINARY RESEARCH

Find out if there is enough information about the topics to fulfill the length and number of sources required for the assignment. Decide which topic is of more interest to you. Save yourself time and aggravation by carefully doing this research now.

PRELIMINARY RESEARCH
                            <u>2/2</u>   <u>X</u>

STEP 3: SELECT TOPIC

Based upon your preliminary research, choose one broad topic.

SELECT TOPIC   <u>2/2</u>   <u>X</u>
<u>Pollution</u>

STEP 4: COLLECT SOURCES

Take out or photocopy sources, such as encyclopedias, on-line magazines, books, periodicals, etc.

COLLECT SOURCES <u>2/5</u>   <u>X</u>

STEP 5: NARROW TOPIC

Skim through your sources for a central theme.

NARROW TOPIC   <u>2/7</u>   <u>X</u>
<u>The Different Types of Pollution</u>

16

	Due by Date	Doing ✔ Done ✗

THE FIRST WRITE

STEP 6:   BRAINSTORM
From the information you have gathered, come up with as many subtopics as possible. Choose the three most relevant.

BRAINSTORM   2/10   ✗
Air Pollution
Water Pollution
Noise Pollution

STEP 7:   THESIS STATEMENT
Write a sentence that states your central theme and what you will say or prove about your topic.

THESIS STATEMENT   2/15   ✗
In order to understand how the environment is being damaged, one must study the air, water and noise pollution of the area. (Be aware of any specific form for a thesis statement that your teacher may require.)

STEP 8:   PRIORITIZE
Decide the order in which you want to present your facts. One way is from strongest to weakest arguments or fact.

PRIORITIZE   2/17   ✗
A. *Air*
B. *Water*
C. *Noise*

STEP 9:   ROUGH OUTLINE
This is a plan for the 5 sections of a paper. Check a teacher's specific requirements.

ROUGH OUTLINE   2/17   ✗
I.   *Introduction including Thesis Statement*
II. *Heading one (details)*
III. *Heading two (details)*
IV. *Heading three (details)*
V.   *Summary/conclusions*

STEP 10: NOTE CARDS
For bibliography and notes from sources.

Unless you are directly quoting, write a paraphrase so you don't accidentally plagiarize.

NOTE CARDS   2/20   ✗

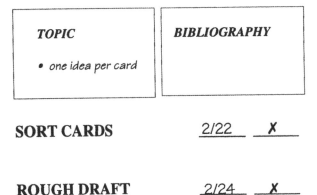

TOPIC	*BIBLIOGRAPHY*
• *one idea per card*	

STEP 11: SORT CARDS
Number cards according to your outline.

SORT CARDS   2/22   ✗

STEP 12: ROUGH DRAFT
Follow your outline and any teacher requirements. Include work cited, end notes and bibliography.

ROUGH DRAFT   2/24   ✗

17

		Due by Date	Doing ✔ Done ✗

THE HOME STRETCH

STEP 13: REVISE
Read your rough draft in its entirety. Does it prove your points and back them up with facts? Are they in the order you want them to be? Does your paper read easily and fluently? Can someone who hasn't done your research understand your position? Check for mistakes in grammar, spelling, and word usage.

REVISE   2/25   ✗

STEP 14: REWRITE
Rewrite using your revisions as your guide.

REWRITE   2/26   ✗

STEP 15: EDIT
Ask someone else to check for errors in capitalization and grammar, organization of your sentences, paragraphs, punctuation, and spelling. Make sure that all rules are followed.

EDIT   2/27   ✗

STEP 16: FINAL COPY
Include all visuals, and cover sheet, etc.

FINAL COPY   2/28   ✗

ACHIEVED GRADE : __A__

CHAPTER 2
LEARNING STYLES

Do you learn better when you are able to hear information or when you are able to see it? Are you a "morning person" or a "night person"? Do you prefer to study by yourself in a quiet room or with a group, with the T.V. on or the stereo blasting? How does your personality affect your learning and study preferences?

All these questions are important to answer if you want to improve your study habits. Students differ from one another in their styles of studying and learning just as teachers differ from one another in their styles of teaching. In this section, we will focus on different learning styles and show you that by understanding how you learn best, your performance in school will improve – and so will your grades.

The strategies presented in this section will help you become more familiar with your best learning style.

- **Understanding How You Learn Best**
- **What's Your Best Study Environment?**
- **Your Personality and Your Learning Style**

Strategy

Understanding How You Learn Best

People learn using three different learning modalities. A learning modality can be either visual (seeing), auditory (hearing) or kinesthetic (touching or moving). While you may use any one or all of these modalities at certain times, most of us use one modality more often than others. That modality is part of your **preferred learning style**.

Directions: **To figure out your preferred learning style, pretend that you have to learn 20 new words and their meanings for a big test. How would you tackle this job? (Check any statements that describe you — you can have none or more than one in any category).**

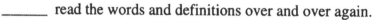

1. I would prefer to:
   _____ read the words and definitions over and over again.
   _____ close my eyes and "see" them in my mind.
   _____ look at pictures that portray the words and their meanings.
   If these are the ways you like to learn new material, you may learn best by seeing, and you are probably a visual learner.

2. I would prefer to:
   _____ recite the words and definitions to myself over and over.
   _____ have the words and meanings taped and then listen to them.
   _____ discuss the meanings with someone.
   _____ listen to the teacher's explanations and recall them later.
   If these are the ways you like to learn new information, you may learn best by hearing, and you are probably an auditory learner.

3. I would prefer to:
   _____ write the words and definitions.
   _____ draw pictures that remind me of the meanings.
   _____ move around as I concentrate.
   If these are the ways you like to learn new information, you may learn best by feeling and moving, and you are probably a kinesthetic learner.

4. Think of other examples which show whether you prefer an auditory, visual, or kinesthetic learning style and write them below.

   _____

   _____

   _____

If you checked off some preferences in each modality, it means that you use more than one modality to learn. Many people are like you and combine what they see with what they hear and write. Use your best learning style whenever you want to be at your most efficient for learning.

Strategy

What's Your Best Study Environment?

Your study environment can affect your learning. Most people become accustomed to studying in a certain setting, around a certain time of day, and in a specific way. They find that they can concentrate best when they are in a comfortable study environment.

Directions: **To understand the type of environment in which you study best, answer the questions below.**

1. I prefer to study:
    _____ early in the day (even get up a little earlier before school).
    _____ in the afternoon.
    _____ in the evening.
    _____ at various times, depending on "what's happening."

2   I prefer to study:
    _____ with background noise such as music or television.
    _____ in almost total quiet.

3. I prefer to study:
    _____ alone.
    _____ in a group.

4. I prefer to study:
    _____ in my room.
    _____ in another room at my home.
    _____ at someone else's home.
    _____ at the library.
    _____ other _____.

5. Describe your ideal study environment. Include a description of the setting, the time of day or night, and whether you prefer studying alone or with others. Explain why you think this type of environment helps you concentrate and study best.

    _____
    _____
    _____
    _____
    _____
    _____

Strategy

Your Personality and Your Learning Style

The way you learn also depends upon your personality and emotional makeup.

Directions: **To understand how your personality influences your study preferences, answer the questions below.**

1. I am a person who:

    _____ shares my ideas and feelings with other people.

    _____ gets new ideas by being part of a group.

    _____ learns by doing.

    If this is you, initiate a small study group before tests, volunteer to demonstrate your ideas, and use computers or science labs. Caution: if you are easily distracted, make sure there is structure within your group and that you can be in situations as free from distractions as possible.

2. I am a person who is:

    _____ uncomfortable when exchanging ideas with others.

    _____ comfortable working alone.

    _____ able to work better alone or with one other person.

    If you do become part of a study group, volunteer to do independent work that you will later share. You may also need to let the group know that rather than giving immediate responses, you may need to take a little time to formulate your answers and then share them.

3. I am a person who:

    _____ likes things in my life to be orderly and well organized.

    _____ is uncomfortable with sudden changes.

    _____ needs to know ahead of time what is expected of me.

    _____ needs to complete tasks ahead of time or at least by the due date.

    If this is you, plan to keep a daily schedule and budget your time in order to do one project at a time. To have a "big picture" keep a semester calendar and write in any activities, tests or projects as you hear of them. When you work with a group, try to team up with people who share your need for systematic planning and early completion.

4. I am a person who:

    _____ likes change and spontaneity.

    _____ waits until the last minute to start a project, but I do get things done on time.

    _____ waits until the last minute to start a project and turns things in late.

    _____ needs to move, so I don't like sitting behind a desk all day.

    Keep a schedule and calendar, but plan extra time to allow flexibility. Highlight due dates and also write in due dates for each step of long-term projects (your Goal Setting Form in Appendix B will be useful for this). Identify the work that must be done first and plan to do it. After you complete each step of a project, check it off. When you complete the entire assignment, cross it off (you'll enjoy the feeling it gives you) and reward yourself.

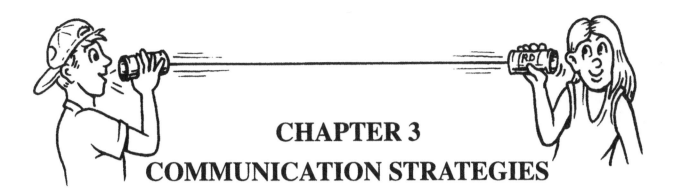

CHAPTER 3
COMMUNICATION STRATEGIES

Now that you've gotten yourself organized and you understand your learning style, it is time to focus on the important skill of communication. Communication is the process of transmitting information from one person or place to another. Typically, we communicate our thoughts and feelings through speech, written language, and behavior.

In school we communicate most often with teachers and other students. Knowing how to communicate effectively with other students enables us to form and maintain relationships, such as friendships. In the same way, good communication between students and teachers enriches the teaching and learning process for both.

In this section we have included several strategies to help you become aware of how to improve your communications skills with teachers and other students. These strategies are:

- **Teacher-Pleasing Behaviors**
- **Understanding Teachers' Expectations**
- **Communicating with Teachers**
- **Cooperative Planning**
- **Communicating with Other Students**

Strategy

Teacher-Pleasing Behaviors

What do students and teachers want from each other? Students want teachers who treat them fairly, and teachers want students who are respectful and ready to learn! We spoke with many teachers who gave us their lists of student behaviors that interfere with their teaching. Why should you want to please your teachers? Think niceness. Think virtue. Think thoughtfulness. Think grades!!

Directions:

Read this list of ten behaviors that bother teachers. Check off any that describe your behavior in the classroom and read the matching teacher- pleasing behavior in italics. Of the ones you've checked, choose the most annoying behavior and plan to change it. Then go on to improve the others. Your teachers will notice and will begin to treat you better also.

Ten Student Behaviors That Bug Teachers and Ten Student Behaviors That Please Them

_____ **Not looking at the teacher.**
When you establish eye contact with the teacher, you look as if you are paying attention.

_____ **Showing up unprepared and not ready to work.**
Prepare your materials early. If you find it hard to remember which materials to bring to class, have a checklist of what to bring to each class.

_____ **Sitting sprawled, head down on the desk, looking as if you're asleep.**
Get more sleep at home. If sitting up straight for an hour hurts, have your back checked. Let your nose face in the direction of where the teacher is teaching.

_____ **Turning in assignments late, or worse, not turning them in at all.**
*Use an assignment book. Plan time each day to do homework with enough time to complete it, then **hand it in**. If long-term assignments are a problem, use your goal-setting sheets to complete assignments by the due dates.*

_____ **Coming into class late.**
Walk to class a little faster. Have shorter hallway conversations. Plan ahead so you don't have to make a locker stop before every class.

_____ **Socializing with friends while important teaching is going on.**
Plan to talk with friends before and after class. Socializing during class is taboo. Warning: So

they don't think you've abandoned them, alert your friends that you'll no longer be talking about next weekend's plans during lectures.

_____ **Asking questions that have nothing to do with a lesson or have already been answered.**
Listen carefully to class discussions. Before you blurt out a question, be sure it has to do with the lesson and hasn't already been answered (this will save you embarrassment).

_____ **Demanding attention when the teacher is busy with other students or other things.**
Unless it's an emergency, be sure the teacher is free to speak with you.

_____ **Being rude to other students or the teacher because their opinions differ from yours.**
If you are rude, even if your point is correct, you'll be perceived as a boor. Listen to other opinions and then disagree with the points, but don't attack the personality of the speaker.

_____ **Doodling or drawing while you need to be listening or taking notes.**
Preview the textbook and listen in class. You'll then be ready to make relevant comments that add to the class discussions.

24

Strategy
Understanding Teachers'
Expectations

The purpose of this strategy is to help you better understand how your teachers teach, what they emphasize, and from where test information is taken. This will allow you to predict what teachers expect of you.

Directions: Under the column "Teacher or Class" write each of your teacher's or class names and as you go down the list check the space that best describes how teachers teach and test.

TEACHER OR CLASS

How Information is Presented

1. Information written on chalkboard or overhead

2. Information presented in lecture and students take notes

Homework Assignments

3. Assigned for practice only and no grade is given

4. Assigned and graded

5. Checked to see if done

Questions on Tests Come From

6. Textbook chapters

7. Textbook questions

8. Teacher's lectures

9. Information found in outside sources

TEACHER OR CLASS

How Teachers Teach and Test

10. Worksheets/packets	10. ___	___	___	___	___
11. Films/Labs	11. ___	___	___	___	___

Test Preparation

12. No review given	12. ___	___	___	___	___
13. Study sheets handed out	13. ___	___	___	___	___
14. Review is done orally in class	14. ___	___	___	___	___

Types of Tests Given

15. Multiple Choice	15. ___	___	___	___	___
16. True/False	16. ___	___	___	___	___
17. Matching	17. ___	___	___	___	___
18. Fill-ins	18. ___	___	___	___	___
19. Essays	19. ___	___	___	___	___
20. Tests vary	20. ___	___	___	___	___
21. Tests written by publisher	21. ___	___	___	___	___
22. Tests written by teacher	22. ___	___	___	___	___

By reading this chart you can "read your teacher" and match what and how you study to each teacher's unique needs. For instance,

- If the teacher lectures, use your notes to study because the information from your notes will be important.
- If homework is assigned and graded, do it well in order to add points to your grade.
- If you know from where teachers get their test questions, concentrate more on those materials.
- If a teacher doesn't review, you will need to review on your own. Pay close attenton in class, because daily lessons may include hints. If a teacher does review, study on your own anyway, but use the teacher's review to narrow down your final studying.

Strategy

Communicating with Teachers

There are times when you will find it necessary to speak with a teacher regarding your school work. Check out the following communication strategies. They will help you approach your teacher in a constructive way and make your discussions positive. (By the way, these communication strategies can be used in many situations and with many different people, not just teachers.)

✔ If you wish to speak with the teacher, first ask when it would be convenient to meet (before school, after school, or during a break, etc.). Then, show up on time. *This shows respect for a teacher's time.*

✔ In advance, because time will most likely be limited, decide the specific points you need to discuss and begin with the most important to you. You may even wish to make a list of the points you need to talk about. *This will keep you organized and let the teacher know that you are serious and thoughtful.*

✔ Eye contact is essential. Be certain to look directly at the teacher without staring. *We all appreciate feeling that the person to whom we are speaking is listening. Eye contact allows you to appear attentive.*

✔ Be prepared for the possibility that you may need to compromise if you and the teacher cannot reach total agreement about an issue. Even if you do not receive the response you wanted, be pleasant and positive. When you are reasonable and fair, you encourage the person to whom you are talking to be reasonable and fair.

Directions: **Role play one or more of the following situations. Role play with a fellow student, friend, or alone. Take one role and then take the other to understand both sides.**

1. You are a student who needs to change a topic for a research paper.

2. You are a student who is asking for extended time to turn in a report.

3. You are a student who is having difficulty in math and needs extra help.

4. You need a written recommendation for a job or student position.

27

Strategy
Cooperative Planning

Even when you try as hard as you can to do well in school, you may sometimes run into problems. When this happens, don't be reluctant to talk to your teacher and plan together.

Directions: **Read the list of common school-related student problems and solutions that teachers and students have thought of to help. If you find that you are having a great deal of difficulty with some of these areas and have been unable to find solutions by yourself, follow these steps:**

1. Make an appointment with your teacher.
2. Together with your teacher discuss your problem areas and fill in the Accommodation Request Form found in Appendix B. If you want to have your parents involved, discuss with them the role they will play.

TROUBLE WITH ORGANIZATION
- encourage student to use a calendar or planner
- write assignments on chalkboard
- allow ample time to copy assignments
- give reminders when assignments are due
- encourage student to purchase second set of books
- color code book covers and notebooks
- encourage use of pocket folders for filing papers
- break down large assignments into smaller parts

TROUBLE COMPLETING ASSIGNMENTS
- use a written contract or work agreement
- use a weekly assignment/grade progress report
- be flexible on late work turned in
- mail home assignments for a week or two
- provide class syllabus to clarify expectations
- give immediate feedback on work turned in and test grades
- meet with student frequently for feedback and direction
- check to see if student understands work assigned
- reduce homework assignment as long as student shows mastery

TROUBLE WITH TEST TAKING
- allow extra time
- test in a distraction-free area
- allow breaks on long tests

TROUBLE TAKING NOTES
- teacher provides outlines for student to fill in
- teacher provides copy of own notes
- share other student's notes
- use tape recorder for missing information

TROUBLE PAYING ATTENTION
- involve student in class discussions
- seat student away from distractions
- cue student when directions are given
- simplify and repeat complex directions

TROUBLE WITH BEHAVIOR
- determine reasons for behavior difficulties by meeting with student, parent, etc.
- post clear rules in classroom
- seat away from friends
- write a behavior contract
- develop a plan with student to help improve behavior

TROUBLE WITH HANDWRITING AND/OR SPELLING
- allow printing instead of cursive
- encourage use of typewriter or word processor
- allow copying of other student's notes
- reduce length of long written assignments
- reduce emphasis on neat handwriting/spelling
- encourage use of spell check systems

OTHER AREAS OF TROUBLE
- _____
- _____
- _____

Exercise
Cooperative Planning Agreement

Directions: After using the accommodations for two weeks, along with your teacher, complete this Cooperative Planning Agreement. This will help you keep track of how well the accommodations you and your teacher agreed to try are working for you.

1. List the accommodations that you and your teacher agree should be tried.

_____

_____

_____

_____

2. As a student, what more can you do to improve in the problem areas you identified?

_____

_____

_____

3. Have the accommodations helped to solve the problems? (Allow 2 weeks before answering.)

_____

_____

_____

4. If there are still problem areas that concern you and your teacher, what else would you agree to try?

_____

_____

_____

_____

Strategy

Communicating with Other Students

School is not only a place for learning; it is a place for meeting other students and making friends. Some of the many ingredients that go into making strong relationships and good friendships involve the ability of a person to show **empathy** and **self-control**, and to display a **cooperative attitude** towards others.

Empathy is defined as the act of showing consideration, sympathy, and sensitivity to the needs of others.

Self-control is defined as the act of controlling one's behavior and emotions under stressful conditions. For example, coping effectively in a difficult situation without becoming upset, depressed, or frustrated. Accepting criticism from others and controlling one's temper are signs of self-control.

Cooperativeness is defined as the act of getting along with others. This includes sharing, taking turns, showing respect for others, etc.

Directions: To evaluate your communications skills with other students, read each of the statements below and rate whether the statement describes you:

Yes   No

Empathy
  1. I show sympathy for others.
  2. I am considerate of others' feelings.
  3. I am a good listener.
  4. I go out of my way to show a helpful attitude to others.

Self-control
  5. I show self-control in difficult situations.
  6. I can accept constructive criticism from others.
  7. I can stay calm when things don't go my way.
  8. It takes a lot for me to get angry.

Cooperativeness
  9. I make friends easily.
  10. I can keep a conversation going.
  11. I invite others to participate in activities.
  12. I compliment others on their work, appearance, etc.

If you had three or more "Yes" answers in each category you probably communicate well with other students. If you had less than three "Yes" answers in any of the categories, try to improve in that area. We have included exercises on the following pages to help you.

Exercise

Increasing Empathy Toward Others

Empathy is the act of showing consideration, sympathy, and sensitivity to the needs of others. Empathy towards someone else can be shown by our words, facial expressions, body language, and our behavior towards others. When we show empathy towards others, we are saying to someone else, "I understand what you're going through and I care about you." We usually show empathy towards others to provide support when someone is going through a difficult time. Needless to say, showing consideration to others and being sensitive to their feelings help build strong relationships.

Directions: **Follow these steps to improve your ability to show empathy towards others:**

1. Figure out how the person is feeling (sad, angy, nervous, worried, etc.)? Watch the other person when they are describing their situation. Notice facial expressions, tone of voice, and body movements. They all give you clues about how this person is feeling.

2. Listen carefully to what the person is saying. Try to follow the content of what they are saying.

3. Decide on ways to show that you understand what the person is feeling such as through a gentle touch or a concerned look or gesture.

4. Review the examples below of empathetic versus nonempathetic statements and actions.

Examples of empathetic statements:

- "You seem upset."
- "I understand how you feel."
- "I can imagine how that must be for you."
- "It sounds like you're going through a rough time."
- "I see what you're saying."
- "I understand."
- "I know what you mean."

Actions or remarks that are nonempathic:

- offering unsolicited advice
- showing disapproval or disrespect
- responding in a judgmental way
- being long-winded
- taking sides
- changing the topic
- looking away while the person is talking
- showing disinterest in the other person
- "If you think you've had it rough, listen to me. My story is worse."

Role Play and Discussion

A good way to practice showing empathy is to role play a conversation. Two or more students can play different parts and be involved in the role playing while other students try to identify empathetic and nonempathetic statements and behaviors that are made.

Example: A student was counting on getting a job in the mall this summer. His application was turned down and he's worried he won't be able to find another job.

Discussing real-life situations when showing empathy helps form and strengthen a relationship.

31

Exercise
Developing Self-Control

Self-control is the ability to control one's behavior and emotions under stressful conditions. Self-control is shown by calmness in our voice and behavior as we react in an even-tempered way without emotional extremes of anger, sadness, or frustration.

Directions: **Follow these steps when faced with a stressful situation.**

1. Give yourself time to "cool off" before reacting.

2. Keep your thoughts and your body calm.

3. Think about your choices and make logical decisions.

Actions you could take to maintain self-control:
- take a deep breath and count to 10 before reacting to a stressful situation
- take a walk; leave the situation for awhile
- try to relax; visualize yourself in peaceful surroundings
- talk sensibly to yourself

Common statetments people say to themselves to keep in control:
- I can work this out.
- I can handle this situation.
- Relax and think this through.
- Stay calm. Breathe easily. Just continue to relax.
- I'm not going to let this thing get the best of me.
- I can stay in control.
- Getting upset won't help anything.
- Don't worry. Things will work out for the best.
- There is no point in getting mad.

Role Play and Discussion

A good way to practice self-control is through role playing and modeling behavior. Two or more students can act out a stressful situation demonstrating different methods of showing self-control. Other students can identify other methods of self-control that can be used.

Discuss examples of real-life situations when self-control could have made for a better outcome in a situation.

Exercise

Cooperativeness

Cooperativeness is the act of showing cooperation to get along with others. Cooperativeness is shown by being helpful, waiting one's turn, sharing, trusting others, listening to others, and following instructions. When we show cooperativeness we are working or playing alongside others in a helpful, positive way.

Directions: **Follow these steps to show cooperativeness:**

1. Determine if the other person may need and want help before offering help. Use verbal, facial, and behavioral cues to judge whether someone needs help (person asks for help, looks puzzled, looks as if he is struggling).

2. When playing a game or sport , show respect for the other person. Follow the rules of the game or sport. Determine who starts and wait for your turn. Congratulate the other person if he won or tell the other person he did well, even if he lost.

3. When working on a project with others, show respect for them. Determine each person's part in the project and make certain to do your share as best you can. Offer help to others, wait your turn when speaking, and be considerate of others' feelings when making comments.

CHAPTER 4
READING COMPREHENSION STRATEGIES

The ability to thoroughly understand what you read is one of the most important skills necessary for school success. Since much of the information in school is communicated either in textbooks, outside readings, notes, or written work, it is essential that you have the ability to understand what you read.

The reading comprehension strategies provided in this section will teach you how to understand concepts by identifying the main ideas and details of a passage.

They include:

- Reading to Understand
- Paraphrasing
- Identifying Signals in a Reading Selection
- Learning New Vocabulary
- 3 Sweeps or How to Really Read a Textbook

Strategy

Reading to Understand

Reading comprehension is an important key to school success! All reading selections consist of three parts: the topic, the main idea and the supporting details. If you learn to identify these three parts within paragraphs, you can improve your reading comprehension.

Directions: **Read the selection in Exercise 1, "Bicycling Again." Then write your answers for Exercise 1 on the lines below.**

Exercise 1

1. Read the title and/or heading to find **who** or **what** the passage is about. That is the **topic**.

2. Read the first two sentences of the first paragraph to find what the author is **telling about the topic**. This is the **main idea**.

3. Read the rest of the paragraph to find the details about the main idea that will answer the questions of **where, when, why and how.** These are the **supporting details** of the main idea.

4. After completing Exercise 1, do Reading to Understand Exercises 2 and 3 on the next page.

Bicycling Again

Bicycling was once a popular sport in the U.S. Today, because people are tired of being bored, fat and addicted to watching T.V., they are making all types of bicycling popular again. "Tour Biking" is enjoying a comeback as solo or small groups of bikers quietly pedal along back roads to enjoy nature's sights. Another way of bicycling is bike racing for people who like speed. They whiz past cars on highways or compete in racing tournaments. A third way of bicycling, mountain biking, satisfies the person who loves both the speed of racing and the beauty of nature. These bicyclists race up mountains and around trees at speeds that would terrify those of us who like our sports slow and level. Because of its new popularity, we are seeing newer and more exciting ways to enjoy the sport as well as more and more bicycles along the roads.

Topic:_____

Main Idea: _____

Supporting Details:

1._____

2._____

3._____

Exercises
Reading to Understand

Directions: Read the selections in Exercises 2 and 3. Write your answers below.

Exercise 2

History of Clowns

The history of clowns can be traced back to ancient times. In ancient Greece, slaves who could make their masters' families laugh were treated better, so smart slaves learned to "clown around." During the Middle Ages, court jesters diverted kings from their problems with their wit and amusing jokes. Even in William Shakespeare's plays during England's Elizabethan period, the "clown" often ruled!

Topic:_____

Main Idea: _____

Supporting Details:

1._____

2._____

3._____

Exercise 3

Life on Mars

They have no antennas or pointy heads emitting death rays, but scientists now suspect that Martians may well be real and living comfortably in secluded parts of the red planet. These hidden residents of Mars are not large organisms, but tiny specks of life smaller than a pinprick. They flourish deep underground in the wet and more temperate regions of the planet's hot interior. Although these Martian microbes resemble the scum on a shower stall, their existence provides enormous possibilities for science.

from Science Times of *The New York Times* by William J. Broad

Topic:_____

Main Idea: _____

Supporting Details:

1._____

2._____

3._____

Strategy
Paraphrasing

Paraphrasing is a powerful way for you to check your understanding of anything that you read.

Directions: **Read the selection "The Blind Do Dream." Then write your answers for Exercise 1 on the lines below.**

Exercise 1

1. Read the title and/or heading to find **who** or **what** the passage is about. That is the **topic.**

2. Read the first two sentences of the first paragraph to find what the author is **telling about the topic.** This is the **main idea..**

3. Read the rest of the paragraph to find the details about the main idea that will answer the questions of **where, when, why and how.** These are the **supporting details** of the main idea..

> **The Blind Do Dream**
> Blind people do dream, they just dream differently than sighted people do. For instance, a person who was born blind sees nothing in his dreams. However, his dreams do have sounds and feelings. On the other hand, a person who goes blind later in life can see in his dreams. His brain recalls how the world looks and can even make new pictures based upon his memory. From what blind people tell us, their dreams of sounds and feelings tell stories that are as real as the sighted person's dreams of pictures.

4. Think of the information from steps 1 - 3. *Say it aloud in your own words*. This is **paraphrasing.**

5. After completing Exercise 1, do Paraphrasing Exercises 2 and 3 on the next page.

Topic:_____

Main Idea:_____

Supporting Details:

1._____

2._____

3._____

Paraphrase: _____

_____

Paraphrasing

Exercise 2

Spoken Language

One of the oldest ways of keeping records is through spoken language. Since man first learned to speak, parents have taught their children the ways of their culture through speech. Stories have been orally passed down through the generations in every culture. In Africa, kings had "rememberers," court officers whose job it was to know the names and deeds of the king's ancestors. Though we lose some of the oral history as time goes by, spoken language is still a rich way for people to record that they were in the world.

Topic:_____

Main Idea:_____

Supporting Details:

1._____

2._____

3._____

Paraphrase:_____

_____

Exercise 3

Beware of Your Perfume

Animals use many forms of communication, and the release of scent is a strong one. Although the most well-known example is the scent used by the skunk to frighten off predators, some odors are used to attract other animals. To let nearby males know that they are ready to mate, females release an odor called pheromones. Males of the species are attracted to the smell and respond immediately. The human species has taken a cue from nature by using pheromone fragrances in women's perfumes such as musk. Although women may wear perfume for their own olefactory pleasure, the woman wearing this perfume should not be alarmed if a love-sick alligator follows her home!

Topic:_____

Main Idea:_____

Supporting Details:

1._____

2._____

3._____

Paraphrase:_____

_____

Strategy

Identifying Signals in a Reading Selection

When you learn to recognize and classify signals used by authors in a reading selection, you will know how to find the information that the author thinks is important. Just as yellow traffic lights signal you to slow down and pay attention to the road ahead, authors' signals alert you to slow down and pay attention to the important information ahead A smart reader "obeys the signals" and becomes attentive to the facts that follow. Often, those are the details put on tests!

Directions: **Read the types of signals below and on the following page.** These and other signals found in your textbooks help you find important information. Become familiar with the type of information they often signal and how an author might use signals to help you decide which ideas to highlight and learn.

SUPPORTING SIGNALS

The ideas that follow these signals support and extend the ideas that came before the signals.

more	furthermore
additionally	moreover
and	1, 2, 3 ....
also	
likewise	

OPPOSING DETAILS

The ideas that follow these signal words oppose or reverse the ideas that were stated before the signal words.

however	although
but	contrary
yet	not
nevertheless	despite
otherwise	

DEFINITIONS

Signals of definitions are not always words but can be commas or dashes. They may also be appositives, or phrases set off by commas to describe the word preceding them.

_____, **or** _____
Ex.   ...trivial, or unimportant
_____, **appositive,** _____
Ex.   ... cranium, the skull, _____.
_____ - _____
Ex.   euphoria - elation

SEQUENCE

These words signal the order in which events occur.

now	first
later	second
before	then
after	finally
yesterday	next
earlier	today
last	tomorrow

SUPERLATIVES

Watch for signals of details that are "super important" because the facts are unique and are worthy of remembering. These facts will often be included on tests.

"most" words...
    Ex. The most important event ...
"-est" words...
    Ex. The largest building in the world ...

ILLUSTRATIONS

With these words, the author signals examples that clarify or further explain information.

for example

for instance

an illustration of this

a case in point

MAIN IDEAS /CONCLUSIONS

These words signal that the idea is an overall concept or result.

in conclusion	thus
in summary	because
the major point	consequently
as a result	therefore

ABSOLUTES

When you are signaled by these words, you know that the information is so rare that it must be learned. These ideas often show up on true/false tests.

all

always

everyone

never

no one

PRESENTATION CUES

Watch for different print styles to indicate important information.

words in bold print

words in italics

words underlined

topics and subtopics printed larger or in different colors

Exercise
Finding Signals in Reading Selections

Directions:

1. Read the text in the box on the right.

2. As you come to a signal or signal word, circle it.

3. Reread the information that comes just after each signal word that you circled.

4. What type of information is signaled?

- ✔ Additional details?

- ✔ Opposing details?

- ✔ Definitions?

- ✔ Main ideas/Conclusions?

- ✔ Sequence?

- ✔ Illustrations?

- ✔ Superlatives?

- ✔ Absolutes?

Hunters and Gatherers

All people of long ago had to get food and shelter just as we do today. However, while we go to the store to buy our food, ancient populations had to rely upon the land.

One way that people got their food was to walk around the area picking what grew wild on trees and bushes, such as nuts and berries. Another way was to eat any plants or roots that could be dug up. Both of these methods are called gathering.

While gathering could supply vegetables, nuts and some fruits, humans also needed to eat meat. Therefore, the cavemen learned to hunt, or find and kill animals such as deer or rabbits.

Because most cavemen got their food by using both methods, they are now known as hunters and gatherers. This was their way of life, or culture. When people develop a culture, they must also devise the tools to keep that culture going. For example, early people invented tools that allowed them to dig up plants more easily, and weapons that allowed them to kill more effectively. As a result of their inventiveness, the early human populations survived and spread their culture throughout our world.

Answers can be found in Appendix A

Strategy
Learning New Vocabulary

Social studies, science, English, math and foreign language classes require you to learn new words and their definitions. This strategy provides a system for you to learn new vocabulary words and will enable you to remember meanings for a long time.

Directions: **Here are two different ways to help you learn new vocabulary. Choose the method that works best for you.**

THE INDEX CARD METHOD

1. Use 3x5 ruled index cards to write unfamiliar vocabulary words or ideas.

2. Look at the word to be learned. Is there something familiar about it? Maybe there is a smaller word within the word. In our example, we recognized the word **APE** in **ape**x.

3. We imagine an ape and then associate it with the meaning of the word, the highest point. We then imagine our ape climbing to the highest point of the mountain.

4. On one side of your card, write the word (APEX) On the other side, write the definition. Then, write a sentence that uses your association to help you understand the meaning.

Index Cards

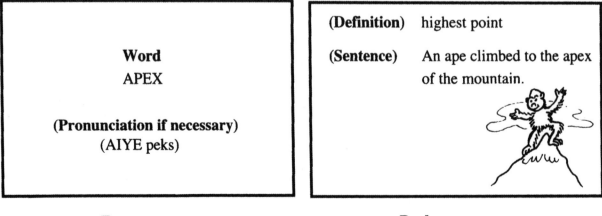

| Word |
| APEX |
| |
| (Pronunciation if necessary) |
| (AIYE peks) |

(Definition) highest point

(Sentence) An ape climbed to the apex of the mountain.

     Front   Back

Strategy
Learning New Vocabulary

THE NOTEBOOK PAPER METHOD:

1. Use a section of your notebook, or keep a separate spiral notebook for all vocabulary.
2. Fold or draw a line down the length of the page about one-third in from the left.
3. Write the vocabulary word in the left column.
4. Write the definition and any examples to the right of the line.
5. To study, fold the right side of page over to cover the definitions or cover the definition with paper. Leave the vocabulary word exposed.
6. Review daily. Include words from previous class tests once a week. This will allow you to master their meanings. Try to use these words in your conversations and writing.

		Subject_____ Chapter_____
1. word	definition, example, explanation, etc.	
2. word	definition	
3. word	definition	fold

Exercise

Learning New Vocabulary – THE INDEX CARD METHOD:

Directions: 1. Read the vocabulary word and its meaning.

2. Draw a picture that will associate the meaning with the word. Make it as funny a picture as you can and give it some action, if appropriate. Don't worry about your artistic abilities; just have fun with this exercise.

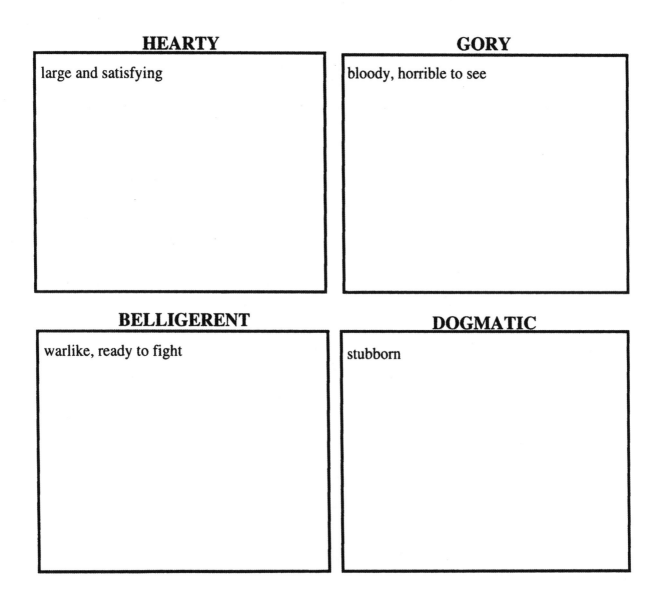

HEARTY

large and satisfying

GORY

bloody, horrible to see

BELLIGERENT

warlike, ready to fight

DOGMATIC

stubborn

Some silly suggestions: Large hearts stacked high on a plate? Gory gorilla? Battling bells? Arguing dogs with "arms" crossed?

Strategy

3 Sweeps or How to *Really* Read a Textbook

To really read a chapter in a textbook and understand what you've read, it is best to use a method of reading comprehension which we call "3 Sweeps." — PREVIEW THE CHAPTER; READ THE STUDY QUESTIONS; and REALLY READ THE CHAPTER. Read the details of each step described below to help you learn the "3 Sweeps" method to read and comprehend any of the chapters in your textbooks.

I. SWEEP 1: Preview the Chapter

Previewing gives you an overview of what is included in the chapter.

A. **Title**: Read the title and ask yourself what you already know about the title and how it fits in with what you previously studied.

B. **Introduction**: Read the introduction to the chapter and ask yourself what it is about (paraphrase aloud).

C. **Headings/Topics; Subheadings/Subtopics**: Read each to gain a general idea of the content to be covered.

D. **Pictures, Maps, Charts**: Look at each to gain additional information concerning the chapter.

II. SWEEP 2: Read the Study Questions

Reading the questions gives you the purpose for reading and provides clues about what details the author thinks are important.

A. Read the study questions at the end of each section, one section at a time.

B. The study questions that begin with these words ask for details:

Who?	——	**asks for people**
What?	——	**asks for events**
Where?	——	**asks for places**
When?	——	**asks for time**
How?	——	**asks for process**
Why?	——	**asks for reasons**

III. SWEEP 3: *Really* Read the Chapter

Use your reading comprehension strategies to read the chapter for the main ideas, details and meanings.

A. Read the first heading/topic to understand the central theme of the section.

B. Read the first paragraph to identify the main idea.

C. After you have read one paragraph, highlight the main ideas and supporting details in yellow. Use the author's signals to help you identify the details that are important. Remember, though, important ideas will not always be introduced by signals.

D. Highlight the vocabulary words and their meanings in a second color. If a definition is not given, look it up and write it in the margin.

E. After each section, paraphrase the main idea and details in your own words. If a section is long or filled with details, paraphrase after each paragraph.

F. Since you have already read the questions at the end of a section, as you come to their answers, write the question numbers next to the line of text.

G. Use the margin of the book to jot notes, definitions, or key words.

If you cannot mark in the textbook, either photocopy necessary pages or, in a notebook, take notes of the main ideas, supporting details, and vocabulary.

Remember: The more active your reading is, the easier it will be to learn and remember the content.

Exercise

Using the 3 Sweeps Strategy in Reading

Directions: **Read the selection "Comets" on the next page using the 3 Sweeps Strategy and answer the questions below.**

1. Define comet.

_____

_____

2. What is the composition of comets?

_____

_____

3. How did Brahe's ideas change people's beliefs about comets?

_____

_____

4. What did Newton discover about a comet's trajectory? How did that make tracking easier?

_____

_____

5. What was Halley's discovery?

_____

_____

6. Why do we see the tail of the comet rather than the body?

_____

_____

7. Describe the two types of comet tails.

_____

_____

8. What was the significance of the Tunguska River area in Siberia?

_____

_____

Answers can be found in Appendix A

Comets

Comets, celestial nebular bodies that revolve around the sun, are familiar to most of us whether it be through movies, television, or newspapers. Nothing, however, can compare to seeing a comet with one's own eyes as it glides past the sun.

For many years, people were mystified by comets. We now know they are like huge snowballs made of ice and earth-like dust that hurl through space.

Early Thoughts

Early astronomers thought comets existed as part of the Earth's atmosphere while others thought that they moved like the planets. In the 16th century, Tycho Brahe found that comets were actually farther away from Earth than Earth's own moon. This dispelled the belief that comets were the property of Earth and triggered many new questions concerning the origins of comets.

To learn more about comets, Issac Newton followed a comet's trajectory and found that it traveled in an elongated orbit instead of a random path as originally thought. Actually, comets are rather predictable. Edmond Halley found this out when he followed what he thought were several comets. Instead, they turned out to be just one, the comet we now know as Halley's Comet. Because of Newton's and Halley's discoveries of comets' paths, scientists are able to predict when a comet such as Halley's will come our way.

The Tail of the Comet

The portion of the comet that we see in the sky is actually the tail, not the body of the comet itself. The tail is easily seen because it points away from the sun (closer to the Earth) due to solar winds of cosmic particles from the sun. The force that gravity has on the comet's gas molecules is one hundred times greater than that of the sun's gravitational pull, so it seems to push the tail away from the sun and into space.

There are actually two types of comet tails. One type is composed of gas or plasma and the other consists of dust. Dust tails are curved and hazy. A comet may actually have a combination of tails, one gas tail and several dust tails, for example.

Collisions

Occasionally, a comet or comet fragment may collide with the Earth, having devastating results, which is just what occurred on June 30, 1908, when a comet collided with an area near the Tunguska River in Siberia. The explosion that followed had the force of an H-bomb. The explosion destroyed trees for miles in all directions, but no crater was formed, and other than some microscopic nodules recovered from the soil, no recognizable fragments from an extraterrestrial object remain. Scientists believe that the explosion was caused by a small comet, meteor, or asteroid that disintegrated in mid-air.

Comets are fascinating objects from space that travel in predictable orbits. When a comet passes by the Earth, we can see the tail if the conditions are right. Occasionally, a comet may collide with the Earth, possibly causing intense damage, but generally, comets are simply following their orbit, just as the planets including Earth are doing.

CHAPTER 5
NOTE-TAKING STRATEGIES

The strategies in this chapter present three different formats for taking notes. Learning all three will enable you to choose the one that is best for you in any situation. You will also learn how to speed up your writing by using abbreviations that make sense. After you master organized note-taking, you will learn how to use your notes to study for tests and even to test your understanding of information before your tests. Finally, you will learn how to figure out what to include in your notes from teachers' lectures and then to combine them with notes from textbooks.

There are eight strategies in this chapter to help you take great notes.

- **Simple Outlining**
- **Mind Mapping**
- **Combo Notes**
- **Using Abbreviations for Speed Writing**
- **Using Recall Questions to Turn Your Notes into Super Study Sheets**
- **Improving Your Listening Power**
- **Taking Notes from Lectures**
- **Adding Textbook Notes to Lecture Notes**

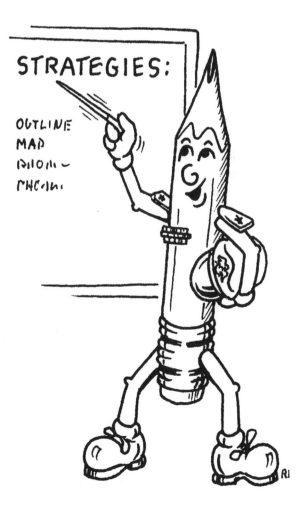

Strategy
Simple Outlining

There is so much information included in textbooks or lectures that you must have a way to include only the most important. This strategy teaches you how to arrange information in your notes in an organized way and quickly identify the main ideas and supporting details of a lecture or reading selection.

Directions:

1. Refer to the sample outline below.
2. The section or chapter title will be the title of your outline.
3. The headings/topics of a chapter are the headings of your outline and are designated by Roman numerals.
4. The subheadings/subtopics of a chapter are the main ideas and are designated by capital letters.
5. The supporting details within main ideas are designated by Arabic numerals
6. The subdetails within the supporting details are designated by lower case letters.

Sample Outline

```
              TITLE
  I. Heading/Topic
     A. Main idea
        1. Supporting detail
        2. Supporting detail
           a. Subdetail
           b. Subdetail
     B. Main idea
        1. Supporting detail
        2. Supporting detail
```

Exercise
Simple Outlining

Directions: Read and highlight the text on the following page, "Pompeii, the City Left Asleep for 1500 Years." Then prepare a simple outline on the form below.

Title

Pompeii, the City Left Asleep for 1500 Years

I. Heading/Topic

   Eruption _____

  A. Main idea

    _____

    1. Supporting detail

    _____

    2. Supporting detail

    _____

  B. Main idea

    _____

    1. Supporting detail

    _____

    2. Supporting detail

    _____

    3. Supporting detail

    _____

    4. Supporting detail

    _____

    5. Supporting detail

    _____

    6. Supporting detail

    _____

II. Heading/Topic

   Discovery _____

  A. Main idea

    _____

    1. Supporting detail

    _____

    2. Supporting detail

    _____

  B. Main idea

    _____

    1. Supporting detail

     a) subdetail

    _____

     b) subdetail

    _____

     c) subdetail

    _____

    2. Supporting detail

    _____

     a) subdetail

    _____

     b) subdetail

    _____

III. Heading/Topic

   City Now Alive _____

  A. Main idea

    _____

    1. Supporting detail

    _____

    2. Supporting detail

    _____

  B. Main idea

    _____

    1. Supporting detail

    _____

    2. Supporting detail

    _____

Answers can be found in Appendix A

Pompeii, the City Left Asleep for 1500 Years

Picture in your mind a major city bustling with 20,000 people. Now, hear a violent explosion of the volcano long dormant within that mountain. As your picture changes to one of death and destruction, would you assume that soon after the eruption ended, people would rush to unearth the treasures of that city? Believe it or not, no one disturbed Pompeii for the next 1500 years! Today you will learn about the disaster of Pompeii and its remarkable aftermath.

The Eruption

In spite of the fact that Pompeii was built upon the hardened lava from a past volcanic eruption of Mt. Vesuvius in Italy, its citizens were unaware of the potential for disaster. They built mansions, traded and enjoyed their lives in that picturesque setting.

In 79 A.D., this long dormant, or inactive volcano erupted again. First, an explosion sounded loudly enough to be heard for miles. Next, lava cascaded down the mountain onto the lavish homes of Pompeii. Then, ash and pumice stone covered the city, followed by a fierce electrical storm that blocked out daylight. Gaseous fumes then killed any remaining life. Finally, in the days after the eruption, rain hardened the pumice stone and ash and buried the city under eighteen feet of paste-like crust.

The Discovery

In 1748, when excavations of the ruins of Pompeii finally began, the preservation was the most remarkable of its time. Remains of 2000 of the 15,000 Pompeians who had perished were found in near-perfect condition. It was found that the ash cover had hermetically sealed, kept out oxygen and other decaying elements, from Pompeii for more than 1500 years. Not only were intact skeletons found, but evidence that the catastrophe took them by total surprise was also discovered. For instance, eggs lay unbroken, jugs held still drinkable wine, and half-eaten meals remained untouched on their plates. The remains of people were found in various stages of action, almost certainly surprised by what was befalling them. An example was a mother and her daughter found holding one another in a last tight embrace. An illustration of misguided priorities was a man discovered standing with his arm outstretched, holding a sword. He had one foot on a pile of gold and five men lay at his feet. The conclusion was that he had slain five men and was threatening the sixth because he was defending his wealth even as he himself was dying.

Once Again, A City Alive With People But . . .

Today, Pompeii is again a bustling city. Three-fifths of the ruins have been excavated and restored, and treasures, both tangible and historical, continue to be uncovered. The magnificence of Pompeii intrigues and draws millions of visitors from around the world. People also again live on the slopes of Mt. Vesuvius. This time, though, its citizens know that another eruption is possible. However, we can be confident that no disaster will lay uncovered for fifteen hundred years; CNN would be there long before then!

Strategy
Mind Mapping

Mind mapping is another way to take notes that you may find fun. It is a visual "map" of how supporting details relate to main ideas. Mind maps are less formal than simple outlines and allow you to use any pattern that works best for you.

Directions: **The look of your mind map is up to you, but these basic directions will make using a mind map easy.**

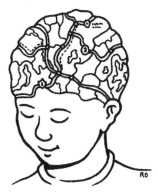

1. First, identify the main ideas and supporting details of what you are reading.
2. Write the subject or topic in the middle of the page. Then draw a circle or box around it.
3. Find the main ideas that relate to the topic.
4. Draw one line from the topic to each main idea and write the main ideas.
5. Write all relevant details on lines that connect to the main ideas they support.
6. Practice mind mapping by following the above directions for the information in your school textbooks.

The figure below is only one of several basic patterns. You will find more on the next pages. These are our maps, but use your imagination to draw your own maps that will help you "see" the relationships and understand the concepts. Have fun.

Sample Mind Map

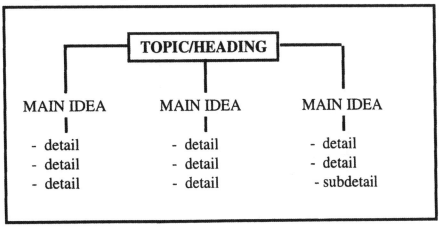

MIND MAPPING MADNESS

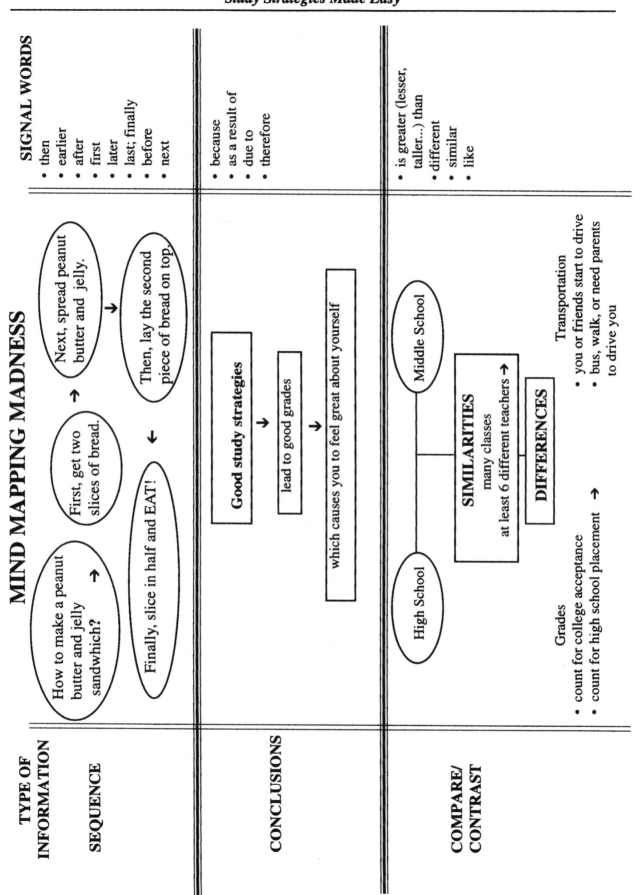

TYPE OF INFORMATION		SIGNAL WORDS

SEQUENCE

How to make a peanut butter and jelly sandwhich?

First, get two slices of bread.

Next, spread peanut butter and jelly.

Then, lay the second piece of bread on top.

Finally, slice in half and EAT!

- then
- earlier
- after
- first
- later
- last; finally
- before
- next

CONCLUSIONS

Good study strategies

lead to good grades

which causes you to feel great about yourself

- because
- as a result of
- due to
- therefore

COMPARE/ CONTRAST

Middle School

High School

SIMILARITIES
many classes
at least 6 different teachers →

DIFFERENCES

Grades
- count for college acceptance
- count for high school placement →

Transportation
- you or friends start to drive
- bus, walk, or need parents to drive you

- is greater (lesser, taller...) than
- different
- similar
- like

MIND MAPPING MADNESS

TYPE OF INFORMATION		SIGNAL WORDS

ILLUSTRATIONS

University School, Saint Thomas and South Plantation are three high schools in Broward County, Florida. Their students attend grades nine through twelve to prepare for colleges or careers.

```
       ┌──────────────┐
  Ex.  │ High Schools │──── Grades 9-12
       └──────────────┘     college prep

  1.  University School
  2.  Saint Thomas
  3.  South Plantation
```

- examples of
- such as
- one of
- some of

CHARACTERISTIC

One feature of in-line skates is the single line of roller blades which helps to give the skater a smooth, fast glide.

```
  ┌───────────────┐
  │ In-line skates │
  └───────────────┘
         │
    ( roller blades ) ──── smooth, fast ride
         │
     single line
```

- one type of
- a feature of

DEFINITION

A strategy, or a plan that you can rely upon each time you meet a similar situation, is easy to learn. For example, a study strategy is one that allows you to plan what you are going to do for each class.

```
                    ( plan )
                      │
                use in similar situations
                      │
                 easy to learn
  ┌──────────┐
  │ Strategy │
  └──────────┘
      │
    ( Ex. )

  Study strats easy to learn
```

- word, **or** definition
  ex. strategy, **or** a plan...
- word, **appositive**,
  ex. study strategy, **a plan to use for each class**, is ...
- word - definition
  ex. strategy - a plan ...

Exercise
Mind Mapping

Directions: Read and highlight the following article. Complete the Mind Map on the following page.

The Brain

What Does Brain Size Actually Mean?

When it comes to the brain, bigger doesn't necessarily mean better. Though an elephant's brain or whale's brain weighs much more than a human brain, scientists say size doesn't count. Instead, scientists compare how much space the brain takes up in comparison to the size of the body it inhabits. For example, an elephant's brain takes up 1/1000 of its body weight, and a whale's brain takes up only 1/10,000 of its body weight. On the other hand, the human brain takes up a sizable 1/50 of a person's body weight. The human brain takes up much more space; therefore, scientists concluded that the proportion of a brain to the amount of space it takes up, rather than mere size, is really what tells how intelligent we are.

What Is the Structure of the Human Brain?

The brain looks like a large gray mushroom with many folds, called convolutions, on its surface. The brain consists of three main parts: the *cerebrum*, the *cerebellum*, and the *medulla oblongata*.

The cerebrum is the largest part of the brain. It lies in the upper region of the skull. Its surface has many deep convolutions and the deepest furrow actually divides the cerebrum into two halves. These halves are called the right and left brain hemispheres. The cerebellum lies in the rear of the skull, just behind the cerebrum. The medulla oblongata, at the top of the spinal cord, connects the brain with the spinal cord that runs down the back of the human skeleton.

What Are the Brain's Basic Functions?

Our brain controls all of our bodily functions. It is the transmission and receipt of messages by the various parts of the brain that allow us to perform these amazing skills.

The cerebrum controls our five senses, determining whether and how we see, hear, taste, smell, or feel. The hemispheres of the cerebrum are truly remarkable because the right hemisphere controls the left side of the body while the left side controls the right side. This means that if you are right-handed, it is the left hemisphere of the brain that is more dominant for you. Many people believe that left-brained people are highly verbal with better math and logic skills while right-brained people have great imaginative and creative abilities. Thus, the cerebrum plays a major role in our lives.

The cerebellum has important functions, as well. It allows us to move smoothly instead of in jerky spurts. It also controls our balance. A dancer's or an athlete's coordination and agility can be attributed to the intact functioning of the cerebellum.

The medulla oblongata controls our basic life functions, such as the involuntary movements of breathing or heartbeats. It also controls our reflexes like sneezing or a quick response to avert an accident. If the cerebrum and cerebellum stop working, a human may survive strictly due to the continued functioning of the medulla.

How Else Is the Brain Important to Our Lives?

Each region of the brain serves a specific purpose and affects specific functions. Damage to the brain, such as from a head injury, results in loss of the skill the damaged area controlled. However, research has proven that if one area is damaged, another area often takes over the job.

It used to be thought that as a person aged, the brain diminished until it barely functioned, often referred to as senility. Today, it has been proven that the brain does shrink in size as we age. However, it has also been proven that we can exercise our brains by using mnemonics, continuing to learn new skills and having new experiences. Even reading and doing crossword puzzles seem to keep our aging memories sharp.

The brain controls every aspect of our thinking, feeling, and behavior. A computer may beat the human brain in speed or the total amount of information it can retain, but it is the brain that is the most intricate and amazing creation known to man.

Exercise
Mind Mapping
The Brain

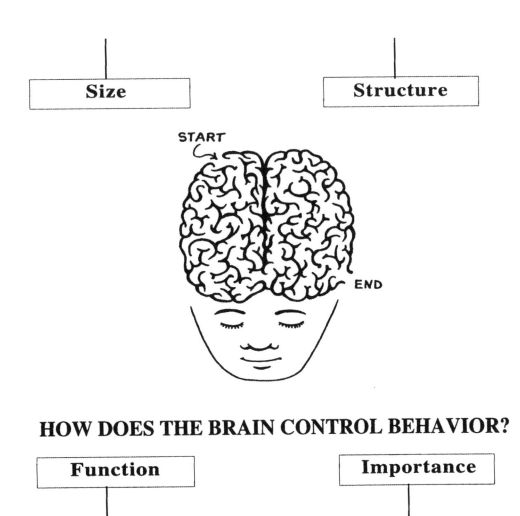

Size		Structure

HOW DOES THE BRAIN CONTROL BEHAVIOR?

Function		Importance

Answers can be found in Appendix A. Also, see if you can find your way through the "brain maze" from start to end.

Strategy

Combo Notes

Since you need to take notes in most classes, using this method will allow you to organize your notes quickly and easily. You can use combo notes when you take notes from your textbooks. A terrific advantage of this style is that you can use it as you listen to lectures with no need to re-write and reorganize later. What a time saver! As you become more proficient taking combo notes, you will create your own symbols, patterns and general style.

Directions: **As with outlining and mind mapping, you will first identify the main concepts and supporting details. Below is a sample of combo notes.**

1. The topic or title is written in the middle of a line and circled.
2. The first main idea is written at the margin and boxed.
3. The supporting detail is indented and designated by a star (☆).
4. The subdetail is indented further and designated by a different symbol.
5. For clear organization margins are kept consistent.

Sample Combo Notes

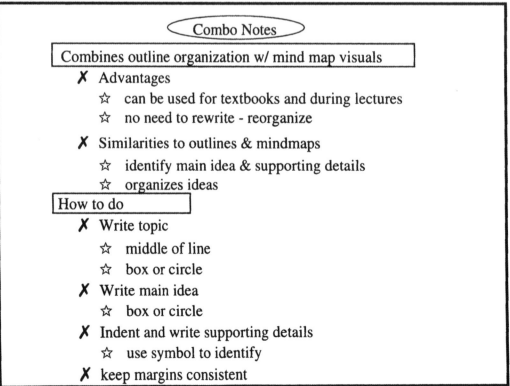

Exercise

Taking Combo Notes

Directions: Read the story of Henry VIII below and write combo notes for this passage on the next page.

HENRY VIII

Historical heads of nations are usually remembered for their leadership abilities or their military conquests. However, when we think of Henry VIII of England, we usually think of his six wives! King Henry's private life changed the course of English history in terms of its politics and religion. His life and times truly could have been a script for a television soap opera.

We begin our tale when Henry first sought to divorce his wife, Catherine of Aragon. Henry had married his wife, who was his brother's widow, soon after becoming king in 1509. After a few years and no male heir, Henry wanted a divorce. He had also become interested in and wanted to marry Anne Boleyn, a maid of honor at his court. One major obstacle for the married Henry was that he was Catholic. This meant that divorce was not allowed, even for a king. No problem! Henry asked the Pope for an annulment on the grounds that it had been wrong for him to marry his brother's widow. To Henry's furor, the Pope refused.

Determined to get his divorce anyway, Henry began steps to solve his problem. He first declared that the Pope had no authority over England and then he secretly married Anne Boleyn. Henry then named Thomas Cranmer as Archbishop of Canterbury; conveniently, the Archbishop quickly approved Henry's annulment.

Finally, with his marital problems settled (for a while anyway), Henry got the Parliament to pass the Act of Separation. This important act finalized England's break from the Church of Rome. It also established the Anglican Church as the official Church of England with guess who as its head. (If you guessed Henry, give yourself an A.) Since the Church of England did allow divorce, Henry had solved his problems and at the same time changed England's religion forever.

Back to Henry's love life! After divorcing Catherine and marrying Anne, Anne had a child. But again, the child was a girl, the wrong sex. Problem: how to get rid of Anne? Solution: charge her with infidelity. Exit poor Anne minus one head. Enter Jane Seymour who died but not before she kindly produced the long-awaited male heir. Henry then married another Anne, this one a German princess. This marriage ended in divorce. (She was luckier than the first Anne and kept her head.) The last two wives were conveniently named Catherine. The former was convicted of misconduct and executed, while the latter and last of Henry's wives actually outlived him.

It is now easy to understand why this fascinating man still remains an imposing figure in history just as he was in real life. And just think – some students actually believe history is boring!

Exercise
Taking Combo Notes (cont.)

Henry VIII

Henry VIII's private life changes English religious history

Henry seeks to divorce 1st wife Catherine of Aragon

✓ Reasons

   ✕_____

   ✕_____

✓ Obstacles

   ✕_____

   ✕_____

   ✕_____

✓ Solutions

   ✕_____

   ✕_____

     -_____

Parliament passes Act of Separation

✓_____

✓_____

   ✕_____

   ✕_____

Henry's 6 wives and what happened to them

1._____

   -_____

2._____

   -_____

3._____

   -_____

4._____

   -_____

5._____

   -_____

6._____

   -_____

Answers can be found in Appendix A

Strategy
Using Abbreviations for Speed Writing

Now that you are taking accurate notes, you are ready to learn the secret of "speed writing" – abbreviations.   You can save some writing time by abbreviating words that you use often.

Directions: 1. Familiarize yourself with the abbreviations below and come up with your own.
2. When taking notes, use key words, not complete sentences.
3. Leave out "little" words, such as: "a," "the," "to," "in," etc. – they won't help your recall.
4. Develop your own system— any abbreviation that you can understand is right.
5. To make sure that you can understand your abbreviation code, write a new abbreviation and the word it represents in a box at the top left corner of the page.

Some Abbreviations That Work

Symbols			*A Few Letters Only*	
#	number		amt	amount
%	percent		assoc	association, associate
$	money, dollars		b/c	because
+	plus, and, more		bio	biology, biography
–	negative, not, no		cont	continue(d)
=	equal		def	definition
≠	unequal, does not equal		eg, ex	for example
>	greater than		etc.	et cetera, also, and so forth
<	less than		govt	government
≥	equal to or greater than		info	information
≤	equal to or less than		intro	introduce, introduction
⇄	to or toward		pp	pages
	away from		re	regarding, about
∴	therefore		s/t	something, sometimes
±	about, more or less		w/	with
@	at, per, each		w/o	without

Strategy
Using Recall Questions to Turn
Your Notes into Super Study Sheets

Making up a recall questions is a powerful way to check your understanding of information found in your textbook and notes. Recall questions ask Who, What, When, Where, Why, and How. They are valuable aids in studying and helping you remember factual information.

The easiest way to understand what recall questions are is to think of the game Jeopardy. In this game, you are given an answer and then must figure out the question. First, after reading, highlighting and/or taking notes on a section or chapter of your textbook, think of the first main concept (the main idea and its supporting details). That is your answer. Next, come up with as many questions as possible for that answer.

The terrific thing about what you've just done is that this is exactly what your teachers do to make up their tests. That means that when you use this strategy, you may find that the questions you made up are the same questions that your teacher makes up and includes on your next test. That fact alone is a good reason to learn and use recall questions. Moreover, research shows that it is important to look over information within 24 hours from the time you receive it and review several more times to improve your recall. If you do this, you will always be prepared, even for pop quizzes. Cramming will be a thing of the past.

Sample recall questions from notes:

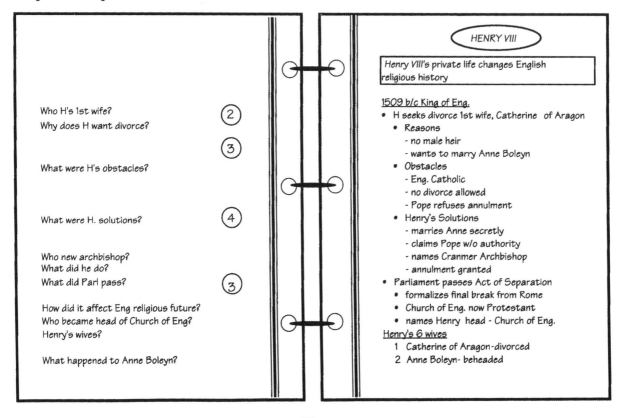

Exercise
Writing Recall Questions

Directions: Before you use recall questions, do this exercise to review your knowledge of the 5Ws + How. Read each information sentence on the right;
then write the letter of its question word on the line next to it. You may
use the same question word more than once.

The question
words are:

A. WHO

B. WHAT

C. WHERE

D. WHEN

E. WHY

F. HOW

1. _____   Halley's Comet will return in 2062.

2. _____   Life was changed after the invention of the
automobile because people and goods were able to
travel greater distances in less time.

3. _____   "Steamboat Willie," starring Mickey Mouse, was
the first animated cartoon movie.

4. _____   The first baseball game is thought to have been
played in Cooperstown, New York.

5. _____   In Africa, people catch flies by stuffing them into
their mouths and enjoying the crunch.

6. _____   Baked Alaska is a dessert of meringue, cake,
and ice cream that can be heated in the oven.

7. _____   John Hanson could be said to be the first
president of the United States.
(Look this up for the "catch")

8. _____   A new scientific discovery has been made.

9. _____   They discovered the existence of life on Mars by
using sensitive probes.

10. _____   The first landings on Mars were two decades ago.

Answers can be found in Appendix A

Exercise
Recall Questions

DIRECTIONS:

1. Read the first facts in the notes for "Laughter is the Best Medicine" on next page. Think of these facts as the **answer** to a test question.

2. Think of questions for that answer. We have started the questions for you beginning with one of the 5Ws + HOW: WHO?, WHAT?, WHERE? WHEN? WHY? or HOW?

3. On the left-hand page (of page 65), across from the first fact, write your first question. (As you become proficient using this strategy, you will be able to write key words or codes rather than complete questions.)

4. If you will need to recall more than one detail, write that number and circle it at the end of the question. This will remind you of how many facts to recall.

5. Read the next concept in your notes and repeat steps 2 - 4.

6. To study this material for a test, you would cover your notes and test yourself by answering each recall question. Reread your notes when you cannot answer a question.

7. Test yourself daily to review the facts of the chapter (yes, even if the teacher hasn't assigned it and you don't know when the real test will be).

8. Remember, if you consistently follow this strategy, you will have the information that your teachers include on tests.

> Suggestion:
> If you are not required to take notes and are allowed to highlight in your textbook, just follow these directions to write your recall questions directly from the information that you highlighted in your textbook. You can write your questions on notebook paper numbering each question. Then write that number by its corresponding answers in the textbook.

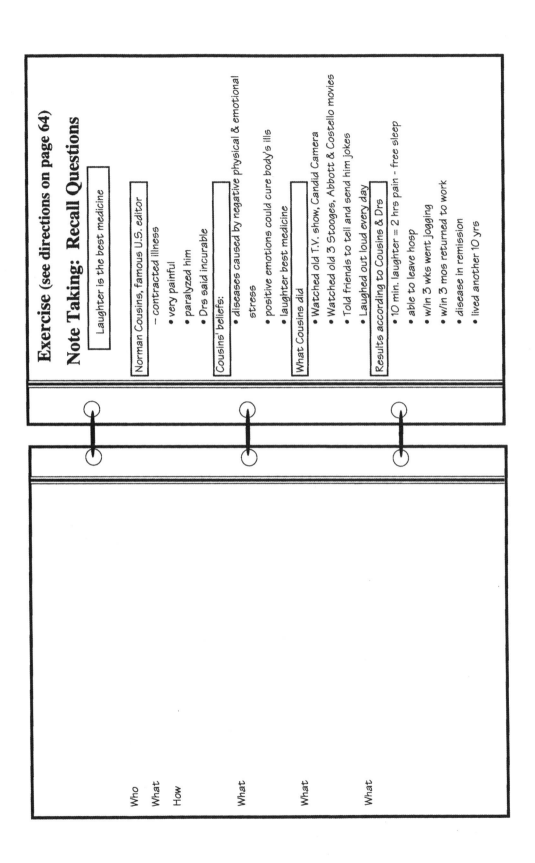

Exercise (see directions on page 64)

Note Taking: Recall Questions

Laughter is the best medicine

Norman Cousins, famous U.S. editor

— contracted illness

- very painful
- paralyzed him
- Drs said incurable

Cousins' beliefs:

- diseases caused by negative physical & emotional stress
- positive emotions could cure body's ills
- laughter best medicine

What Cousins did

- Watched old T.V. show, Candid Camera
- Watched old 3 Stooges, Abbott & Costello movies
- Told friends to tell and send him jokes
- Laughed out loud every day

Results according to Cousins & Drs

- 10 min. laughter = 2 hrs pain - free sleep
- able to leave hosp
- w/in 3 wks went jogging
- w/in 3 mos returned to work
- disease in remission
- lived another 10 yrs

Who
What
How

What

What

What

Strategy

Improving Your Listening Power

When a teacher talks, it pays to listen. Why? Because when a teacher is lecturing, you are getting the information that is considered the most important to learn. Therefore, it will probably be included on future tests. This strategy will help you to identify clues that lecturers give you when they think some information is particularly important.

Lecturers use three types of cues to let you know which facts are important. Therefore, pay close attention to the information that follows these cues.

1. **VERBAL CUES:**

    Review the signals listed on pages 38 and 39 because the same signal words that are used in textbooks are used in lectures to indicate important information.

2. **PRESENTATION CUES:**

    While a textbook uses presentation cues such as bold type to indicate important information, the lecturer may:
    * say certain words or phrases slower, faster, louder, or softer.
    * repeat key phrases.
    * spell important words.
    * write key concepts on the board.

3. **BODY LANGUAGE CUES:**

    Pay attention if the lecturer changes the usual movement of hands, head or body. Since body language cues are often subtle, become aware of each teacher's unique and unusual use of body language. You may be surprised at how often a change of routine can cue what the teacher thinks is important.

Directions:

1. Pay careful attention to all of these cues, and note the information they signal.

2. Preview your textbook chapter the night before the lecture so that you have an idea of what to listen for. This will help you decide what to include in your notes.

3. Do the exercise on the following page to improve your listening power.

Exercise
Improving Your Listening Power

Exercise 1
Listen to a television newscast. As you listen, write any verbal or presentation cues the speaker is using. As you watch, write any body language cues the speaker is using.

Newscast channel and/or speaker: _____**Date**:_____

CUES:

Verbal: _____

_____

_____

_____

Presentation: _____

_____

_____

_____

Body language: _____

_____

_____

Exercise 2
For one day, choose a class to watch for the teacher's lecture cues. As you listen, write any verbal or presentation cues the speaker is using. As you watch, write any body language cues the speaker is using.

Class or teacher: _____

CUES:

Verbal: _____

_____

_____

_____

Presentation: _____

_____

_____

_____

Body language: _____

_____

_____

Strategy

Taking Notes from Lectures

Think of a lecture as a teacher's gift to you. Why? The teacher has already done the work for you by researching the entire subject, pulling out the most important parts and then handing it to you in a brightly wrapped gift – the lecture. A word of caution: while you will get a lot of information from the lecture, there may be important details found only in your textbook, so be sure to read it.

How can you prepare to take notes?
- Preview your textbook chapter the night before the lecture so that you have an idea of what to listen for and to include in your notes.
- Before you walk into the classroom, decide which note-taking method you will use to keep your notes organized: outline, mind map, or combo.
- In class, concentrate on what is being said and be aware of cues that signal important information. Remember, though, that sometimes important information is not always preceded by cues.

What can you do to keep up?
- If you find the teacher is speed-talking while you're crawl-writing, learn to listen and write at the same time.
- Listen until you understand what the idea is, then begin writing the idea in your own words. Don't worry that you can't write every word the teacher says; you're better off. If you are able to write a paraphrase, you probably understand the lecture.
- Abbreviate to speed up your writing.
- Skip lines between each concept and write one idea per line.

What if you get lost along the way?
- If you know you missed something, skip a few lines and "tune back in." Later, ask your teacher or a student to fill you in on what you missed.
- If you don't understand something the teacher said, write a question mark in the margin and check in your textbook for further clarification. The information you've missed may be explained in the chapter. If not, ask for an explanation during the next class. This will allow you to show that you are an interested student, which is a definite teacher-pleasing behavior.

What if taking notes is too difficult?
- You may have to put in more time and practice before you master note-taking. However, there are a few people for whom taking lengthy notes is too difficult. If you are one of these people, you still have several choices. Speak with your teacher. Perhaps with some cooperative planning, modifications can be made such as: getting permission to tape the lecture; asking the teacher for his/her notes; getting copies of the notes of a student who takes good notes, etc.
- Remember that if you are able to get note-taking modifications, you must still take your own notes. Your options are only to supplement your notes.

Strategy

Adding Textbook Notes to Lecture Notes

Sometimes important information in a textbook is omitted from a teacher's lecture. If text information will be included on a test, use this strategy to add that information to your lecture notes.

Recall Questions

Write questions about lecture and textbook facts.

Notes from Textbook

Include only information not already in lecture notes.

Class Lecture Notes

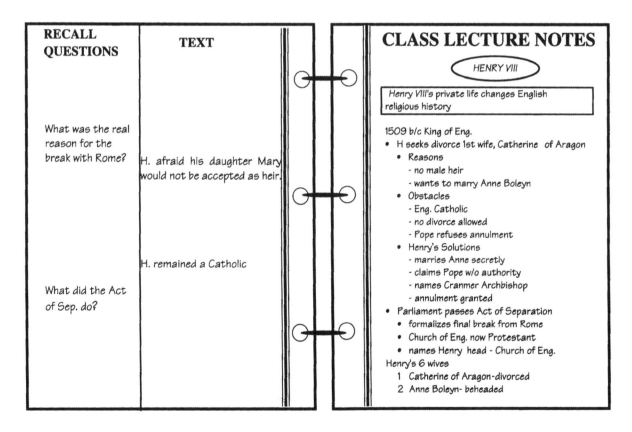

RECALL QUESTIONS | **TEXT**

What was the real reason for the break with Rome?

H. afraid his daughter Mary would not be accepted as heir.

H. remained a Catholic

What did the Act of Sep. do?

CLASS LECTURE NOTES

(HENRY VIII)

Henry VIII's private life changes English religious history

1509 b/c King of Eng.
- H seeks divorce 1st wife, Catherine of Aragon
  - Reasons
    - no male heir
    - wants to marry Anne Boleyn
  - Obstacles
    - Eng. Catholic
    - no divorce allowed
    - Pope refuses annulment
  - Henry's Solutions
    - marries Anne secretly
    - claims Pope w/o authority
    - names Cranmer Archbishop
    - annulment granted
- Parliament passes Act of Separation
  - formalizes final break from Rome
  - Church of Eng. now Protestant
  - names Henry head - Church of Eng.
Henry's 6 wives
  1 Catherine of Aragon-divorced
  2 Anne Boleyn- beheaded

Reminder: If you review your recall questions nightly, you will be prepared for the test without last-minute cramming and panic!

CHAPTER 6
MEMORIZATION STRATEGIES

The most thorough reading, highlighting, note-taking, and questioning for recall will not result in good test scores unless you are able to remember the information during the test. In this section we will introduce ten different memory strategies that can help you recall important information.

We store information in three different ways:

IMMEDIATE MEMORY allows us to repeat facts or follow directions that we have just seen or heard. However, we do not retain them.

SHORT-TERM MEMORY allows us to briefly retain facts. This is what is working when we cram for a test.

LONG-TERM MEMORY allows us to retain and much later recall information. If we've intended to learn, rehearsed and repeated information, we more easily recall it for cumulative exams like finals.

Although we don't consciously direct information to any of these storage systems, our brain seems to know how long the information needs to be stored and takes care of the process on its own. We can help the brain store information by using a number of strategies that will be explained in this section.

- **Remembering Requires Understanding and Planning**
- **Memory Techniques**
- **Memorizing by Using Acrostics and Acronyms**
- **Memorizing by Using Charting and Visual Emphasis**
- **Memorizing by Using Visualization**
- **Memorizing by Using Association**
- **Memorizing by Linking Information**
- **Memorizing by Using Rehearsal**

Strategy
Remembering Requires Understanding and Planning

Understand, then Memorize

It is easier to remember information we understand. Look at the following information. Which is easier to memorize?

       1. XKY, TWI, PLX, ZYK, JYL
       2. Six, can, are, jog, who
       3. Ten, kids, buy, ice, cream

Is your answer #3? That's because this information has meaning, or makes sense to you, and it would be easier to "file" in your memory and to recall later.

Be Selective, then Memorize

Selectivity is a must because it is impossible to learn every fact. So, before you begin to memorize, decide which facts to learn. These are ways to help you decide:

   ✍ Past tests tell you the type of information a teacher emphasizes, such as
      1. facts – people, places, events, and dates.
      2. vocabulary
      3. general concepts
   ✍ Notes of a teacher's class lecture let you know what to study since the teacher has already pulled out the important information.
   ✍ Review or study sheets are a teacher's way to let you know what will be on a test.
   ✍ Oral reviews are the teacher's hints to you.

Plan to Use a Memory Technique

Plan how to organize and store information by choosing the memorization techniques found on the following pages. Regardless of the techniques you use, repetition and review over several days will be necessary to transfer the information into short-term or long-term memory.

Strategy
Memory Techniques

Think of how you learn best. If you can recall what you see better than what you hear, you are a visual learner. If you recall what you hear better than what you see, you are an auditory learner. If you need to write things down in order to remember them, you are a kinesthetic learner. Many of us combine what we do in order to learn. Whatever your personal learning style, there are memory techniques that will make learning easier for you. Remember, though, repetition is a necessary evil in order to remember information regardless of the techniques employed. The greater the understanding, the easier the memorization becomes. Practice sessions should be spaced over several days. DO NOT CRAM!

Read the chart below to help you choose techniques that will work best for you.

__Techniques__	__Learning Style__		
	Auditory	**Visual**	**Kinesthetic**
1. acrostics	✔	✔	✔
2. acronyms	✔	✔	✔
3. charting		✔	✔
4. visual emphasis		✔	✔
5. visualization		✔	
6. association	✔	✔	
7. word linking	✔	✔	✔
8. story linking	✔	✔	✔
9. rehearsal	✔	✔	✔

Strategy

Memorizing by Using Acrostics and Acronyms

1. SILLY SENTENCES (Acrostics)

It is easier to memorize a long list if it makes sense the way a sentence does. To make a list meaningful, use this mnemonic. Use the first letter of each word to be memorized to make a sentence (the sillier the better).

EXAMPLE: To memorize the planets in their order from the sun:
  Mercury - Venus - Earth - Mars -Jupiter
  Saturn - Uranus - Neptune - Pluto
  USE: **My Very Educated Mother Just Served Us Nine Pizzas**

EXAMPLE: To learn how living things are classified and divided into groups:
  Kingdom - Phylum - Class - Order - Family - Genus - Species
  USE: **King Plays Chess On Fat Girl's Stomach**

EXAMPLE: To memorize the order of mathematical operations:
  Parentheses, Exponents, Multiply, Divide, Add, Subtract
  USE: **Please Excuse My Dear Aunt Sally.**

EXAMPLE: To learn the countries of Central America:
  Belize, Guatamala, El Salvador, Honduras,
  Nicaragua, Costa Rica, Panama
  USE: **Big Girls Eat Hot Nacho Chips Plain**

2. WACKY WORDS (Acronyms)

Sometimes, you will not need to use a whole sentence to help you memorize. The acronym is a shorter version of the acrostic. Like silly sentences, use the first letter of each concept to be learned to form one word. The word or words do not have to be real words as long as they are easy for you to remember.

EXAMPLE: To memorize the order of operations:
  Parentheses, Exponents, Multiply, Divide, Add, Subtract
  USE: **PEMDAS**

EXAMPLE: To memorize the spectrum of colors:
  Red Orange Yellow Green Blue Indigo Violet
  USE: **ROY G BIV**

EXAMPLE: To memorize the Great Lakes:
  Huron, Ontario, Michigan, Erie, Superior
  USE: **HOMES**

Strategy

Memorizing by Using Charting and Visual Emphasis

3. CHARTING

This technique works when you are asked to learn and compare the characteristics such as the list below. It is also a powerful device when you need to compare and contrast the ideas, characteristics, or theories in literature, history, science, math, etc. Charting allows you to easily see the information and then recall the chart and its contents during a test.

EXAMPLE: To classify vertebrates according to common attributes:
USE: Chart each concept to graphically see comparisons and contrasts.

	VERTEBRATES		
	Blooded	**Breathing**	**Reproduction**
FISH	cold	gills	external
AMPHIBIANS	cold	gills, lungs	external
REPTILES	cold	lungs	external
BIRDS	warm	lungs	external
MAMMALS	warm	lungs	internal

4. VISUAL EMPHASIS

Highlight, circle, box, or color portions of information to emphasize the key part or parts that are difficult for you to learn.

EXAMPLE : To learn the process of photosynthesis highlight the key words:
USE: Green plants combine **WATER** and **CARBON DIOXIDE** and **ENERGY** from sunlight **TO MAKE FOOD.**

EXAMPLE : To learn the main points of notes or text, box in key concepts:
USE: | John Hanson may have been our first president. |
  • elected 1st "President of the U.S. in Congress Assembled"
  • 8 years before Geo. Washington elected

Strategy

Memorizing by Using Visualization

5. VISUALIZATION

Research tells us that we can enhance our memory by actually drawing a picture or visualizing something that we want to recall at a later time.

◆ To visualize information in textbooks or notes, close your eyes and form a picture of the page. Visualize the heading, **boldface print,** *italics*, and general format of information to remind you of the sequence of ideas.

◆ To visualize vocabulary words and their definitions, look at the word you are to memorize. Ask yourself if there is a part of the word that *looks* or *sounds* familiar to you, that you can *"see."* Use that association to draw (or imagine if you don't draw) as silly a picture as you can. Then, make your picture *do* something that directly relates to the meaning of the word.

EXAMPLE: You must learn the word **insuperable** for a vocabulary test. One student used this visualization strategy. He pictured in his mind a soup can trying to jump over a wall. The soup can could not <u>come over</u> the wall. He used this picture to remember that insuperable means "unable to overcome." Drawing a picture can help you remember the definition even more clearly.

The same student used this visualization strategy to remember the definiton of the word **inclination** which means "a liking or leaning toward." He pictured a nation leaning or sliding toward. He drew a quick sketch of this to reinforce the meaning of the word in his memory.

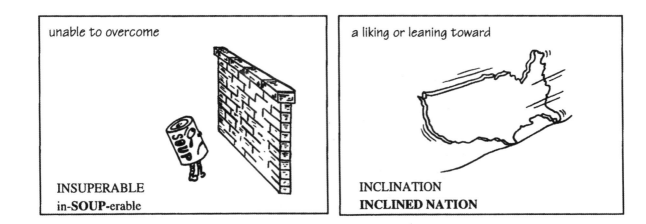

unable to overcome	a liking or leaning toward
INSUPERABLE in-**SOUP**-erable	INCLINATION **INCLINED NATION**

Visualization, cont.:

Visualization can be used to memorize facts as well as vocabulary words. When asked to learn capitals of different countries, a student used visualization to help remember that Brussels is the capital of Belgium. He associated the word Brussels to brussel sprouts and the word Belgium to belgian waffles. He formed a visual picture in his mind of a dish of bright green brussel sprouts atop belgian waffles.

Visualization can also be used to remember math facts, such as liquid measurement. For example, if you want to remember how many cups, pints and quarts are in a gallon, you can use the visual image below to remember that there are four quarts, eight pints, and sixteen cups to a gallon.

Strategy

Memorizing by Using Association

6. ASSOCIATION

When you need to memorize separate facts, find a way to associate them and use that association in a phrase, a sentence, a rhyme, or a story.

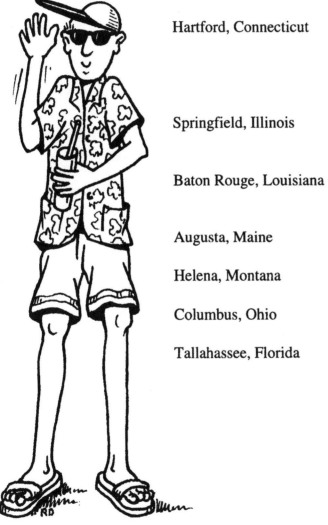

EXAMPLE :	To learn capitals of U.S. states:	*USE:*
	Juneau, Alaska	Too cold to go to **Alaska** except in **June**.
	Hartford, Connecticut	**Connected hearts**
	Springfield, Illinois	You can't **spring** out of bed if you're **ill.**
	Baton Rouge, Louisiana	**Louis** puts **rouge on** with a **bat.**
	Augusta, Maine	It's **mainly** hot in **August**.
	Helena, Montana	**Helen** climbs a **mountain**.
	Columbus, Ohio	**Columbus** said, "**Oh, Hi!**"
	Tallahassee, Florida	**Tall Floridian**

Strategy

Memorizing by Linking Information

7. WORD LINKING

When you are required to learn a list of facts, use word linking to form associations that link one idea to the next. This strategy will also enable you to memorize information in sequence for tests, essays, or even oral presentations.

FOR EXAMPLE: To memorize the names of the inert elements on the Periodic Table, HELIUM, NEON, ARGON, KRYPTON, XENON, and RADON.

USE THIS METHOD: Make up a word link similar to the one we did below:

- Associate the first word or fact (in this case, HELIUM) with something you already know – a big, bright helium balloon.
- To link helium to the next word, NEON, think of the helium balloon holding up a wildly colored neon sign.
- To link the neon sign to the next word, ARGON, associate argon with the state of Oregon (look up the shape on a map. Imagine Oregon on the neon sign being held up by a helium balloon.
- The next word is KRYPTON. If you have seen Superman, you will remember that he is made helpless by kryptonite, so imagine Superman on the ground under the neon sign holding *kryptonite*.
- To link this to XENON, imagine that the kryptonite is refueling at an Exxon (looks like xenon) gasoline pump and Superman is holding on to the Exxon pump.
- To associate xenon with RADON, imagine the xenon (Exxon pump) zapped by a huge red ray gun (radon).

8. STORY LINKING

If the information you need to learn is just too long, don't try to learn it all at once. Break up the information to be learned into smaller chunks and then link them together in a story.

FOR EXAMPLE: To memorize the first ten U.S. Presidents

USE THIS METHOD: Make up a story that links the first to the second, the second to the third, and so on until you reach the last one. The following sample story can be memorized three names at a time.

[Think of George Washington not only as our first president, but as somewhat of a klutz, always cutting himself; and so our story ...]

When **Washington** cut down the cherry tree, he also cut his **Adams** apple. Blood gushed all over his **Son, Jeff** (Jefferson). Jeff was **Mad** (Madison) at the **Money** (Monroe) fixing another **Adams** (another Adams) apple would cost. Along came the nicer **Son, Jack** (Jackson) to help, but his **Van Burned** (Van Buren) while **Hurrying** (Harrison) to the hospital, so they just temporarily **Tied** (Tyler) a bandage around the bloody wound.

Disclaimer: None of the persons named above bear any resemblance to their historical counterparts. That's part of the fun; the wild characteristics or actions you attribute to anyone are only limited by your own imagination.

Strategy

Memorizing by Using Rehearsal

9. REHEARSAL

Just as an actor rehearses his lines for a play until he knows it well enough to perform, a student rehearses information for a test until he knows it well enough to perform. Rehearse information to be remembered using your strongest learning style.

If you are an **auditory learner**, you remember better what you hear.
> Rehearse by:
> * repeating the information to be memorized out loud.
> * using a tape recorder to listen later for reinforcement.

If you are a **visual learner**, you remember better what you see.
> Rehearse by:
> * reading the information.
> * visualizing associations.
> * drawing pictures.

If you are a **kinesthetic learner**, you remember better when you can do something.
> Rehearse by:
> * jotting down brief notes.
> * outlining, mind mapping or taking combo notes.
> * drawing pictures.
> * using objects that symbolize the information.

If you are a **combination learner**, you remember better by combining two or more of the above strategies. Rehearse by choosing the combination of strategies that works best for you. The content of the information will determine your strategies.

CHAPTER 7
TEST-TAKING STRATEGIES

As you know, besides projects such as written papers, oral reports, and homework assignments, good test grades are essential to your overall grades in class and your success in school.

In this section you will learn specific strategies to help you earn the best grades on tests. The strategies you have already learned will have prepared you well for tests. In this section, Test -Taking, you will learn about five different types of tests that teachers usually give and the strategies you can use to succeed on each type. We will also give you some tips about how you can use old tests to help you prepare for new ones and help you prepare for larger tests such as midterms and final exams.

The following strategies will be found in this section:

- **Reading Directions Carefully**
- **Taking Objective Tests**
- **Taking Matching Tests**
- **Taking True-False Tests**
- **Taking Fill-In Tests**
- **Taking Multiple Choice Tests**
- **Check What You Know About Taking Tests**
- **Taking Essay Tests**
- **How to Begin the Essay**
- **Subjective Testing**
- **Making Old Tests Work for You**
- **Studying for Midterm and Final Exams**

Before you begin to review these strategies, take Today's Test on the next page.

Today's Test

Name: _____

Directions:

    1. Read all the directions before you begin.

    2. Write the city and state where you live.

    3. Cross out all vowels.

    4. Count the number of letters remaining.

    5. Multiply that number by your age.

    6. Divide by your grade. Round off to the nearest whole number.

    7. Add the number of hours in a day.

    8. Subtract the number of letters in your first and last name.

    9. Divide by two.

    10. Directions from two to nine do not need to be done.

Work space:

Strategy

Reading Directions Carefully

If you did no work on the exercise "TODAY'S TEST" on the preceding page, congratulations!! You know the number one rule of test taking.

If you did some or all of the work before you realized the trick, you should now feel good because you now know what good test takers know: **You must read all directions before you begin working!**

Imagine that you are attempting to go to a location in an area of town that you've never been to before (a new friend's house, the mall?). If you have been given no directions, no map, how will you get there?

You may say that you'd stop strangers along the way to ask directions. This strategy could work. But it would certainly make your trip harder and maybe even frustrating. You might even feel like giving up before you reach your destination. However, if you get directions before you start out and then follow the directions, you certainly lessen your chances of getting lost and frustrated, and you increase your chances of successfully and more easily reaching your goal.

Taking tests is similar to going on a trip. You want to know *before you begin* how to take the shortest and best route to reach your destination. When taking a test, you'll want to read directions carefully to earn the best grade. Therefore, it makes sense to read and follow directions when you take a test.

Study Habits Checklist

The way you study for tests has a lot to do with your grades. While your study skills may be good, streamlining them so that you are even more efficient will let you earn grades that are even better! Use this checklist to see how efficiently you are studying now. Then use your answers to help you plan for the next test.

Directions: **Think of a recent test you took in a content area course (e.g., science or history) and evaluate the way you studied for it. (If you can have the test to review, use it to answer these questions.)**

1. When did you study for the test?
   _____ from the time the chapter was assigned.
   _____ over several (more than 2) nights.
   _____ the night before the test.
   _____ just before the test.
   _____ not at all.

2. What study techniques did you use?
   _____ I looked over the chapter.
   _____ I read my notes.
   _____ I read the content over and over.
   _____ I wrote notes of the material.
   _____ I used recall questions for review.
   _____ I used at least three different memory techniques.
   _____ I made up sentences to memorize.
   _____ I taped, then listened to the material.
   _____ Someone quizzed me.
   _____ I thought I already knew it and did nothing.

3. After you studied, did you feel confident that you knew the material? _____ no _____yes

4. Before the test, did you feel nervous? _____ no _____yes

5. Did you recall the information during the test? _____ no _____yes

6. Were there any types of questions you found particularly difficult? _____ no _____yes
   If yes, which? ___ multiple choice ___ true/false ___ fill-ins, ___ matching ___essay

7. If you got your test grade was it _____better than,_____ worse than, or_____what you expected?

8. Which strategies seem to be the most helpful? _____
   _____

9. Which strategies should I use to be better prepared for the next test? _____

Strategy

Taking Objective Tests

Objective tests are the most popular type given by teachers. There are four types of objective tests:

- ✏ matching
- ✏ fill-in-the-blanks
- ✏ true-false
- ✏ multiple choice

Objective tests require that you recall specific factual information such as definitions, dates, people, places, and events. Objective tests have either a right or wrong answer. Usually these answers are readily available in your textbook, lecture notes, or additional readings assigned by the teacher. Your recall questions are an excellent review for objective testing.

When you take any objective test, follow these general rules:
1. Determine how many questions there are and how much time is allowed.
2. Estimate how much time to spend on each question.
3. When beginning the test, **always read all the directions.**
4. Answer the easiest questions first. Later, go back to complete the more difficult ones.
5. Unless you are penalized for wrong answers, make an educated guess. Don't leave any questions blank.
6. If you are taking a scantron type test, be sure to bubble in the answer sheet correctly.

Each type of objective question has its own rules. The following strategies can be very beneficial when you follow them. Plan to practice and then apply these strategies for every objective test you take.

Strategy

Taking Matching Tests

Matching tests usually require you to match words in one column with related phrases in another column. Matching is often used for vocabulary, people and events in history, or scientific occurrences. Follow the strategies listed below to make a matching test an easy match for you.

1. Read all directions.

2. Count all choices in each column. If one column has more choices than the other, work the column with fewer choices first. You won't waste your time trying to match an answer that doesn't have a match. This is a trick on matching tests called a "ringer." Don't fall for it.

3. If both columns have the same number, first work the column with the explanations because they may contain clues. If you have to reread, it is easier to reread the shorter matches.

4. When you choose an answer, cross it out so you will not have to read the choice again.

Directions: **Take this matching test below using the above strategies.**

A	**B**

_____1. Baseball

_____2. Football

_____3. Soccer

_____4. Tennis

_____5. Skiing

_____6. Swimming

A. Use your head, use your feet, but in this sport, don't touch the ball with your hands.

B. Does it sound like a sport if it has tees, birdies, eagles, woods, and irons?

C. If you think a lap is only what happens when you sit, you've never tried this sport.

D. If stealing is a sin, how come players of this sport steal bases all the time?

E. This sport can leave you cold atop a mountain with only poles to help you down.

F. In this sport, even if you smash someone, you could still be in love.

G. A math problem: Explain how this sport takes three hours to play four fifteen-minute quarters.

Answers can be found in Appendix A

Strategy

Taking True-False Tests

True-false questions are really statements that are either entirely true or not true. Follow these strategies when taking a true-false test. They will be easy to do.

1. Read all directions.

2. True/false questions often contain clues to help determine whether they are true or false. Some key words make the statement always true, sometimes true, or never true.

   • Since there are few absolutes in this world, words that mean "all" or "never" will *usually* signal that the statement is false. Become familiar with the following words:

   ALL   ONLY

   ALWAYS NONE

   EVERY   NEVER

   • Some words are more often found in true statements:

   SOME   MAINLY

   USUALLY OFTEN

   SELDOM   EXCEPT

   SOMETIMES RARELY

   PROBABLY

3. Look carefully at the sequence of the statements. The facts may be accurate, but the order may cause the statement to actually be false.

   Example: The president *following* Richard Nixon was John F. Kennedy.

4. Sometimes a true statement will be reworded so that positive words replace negative ones or vice versa.

   Example: If the textbook read, "The soldier *did not wish* to return to the frontlines," but the test statement reads, "The soldier *wanted to* get back to the battle front," the statement is false.

5. In order to be true, the entire statement must be true. Therefore, if the entire statement is true, mark true. If any part of the statement is false, mark false.

Exercise
True-False Tests

Directions: **The following statements include information from some of the academic subjects you study in school, so you should be familiar with most of the content. Read the sentences and if the statement is true, write T on the line. If the statement is false, write F on the line.**

1. _____   All musicians can read music.

2. _____   It seldom snows in tropical climates.

3. _____   George Washington was elected president after Abraham Lincoln.

4. _____   There is only one meaning for the word "play."

5. _____   In the United States, presidential elections are held every six years.

6. _____   Verbs include action words such as: run, play, sing, dance.

7. _____   Computers can always out-think people.

8. _____   Studying never helps improve grades.

9. _____   Most teachers are right-handed.

Answers can be found in Appendix A

Strategy
Taking Fill-In Tests

Fill-in-the-blank questions are complete statements with a key word or phrase missing. When you take a fill-in-the-blank test, your job is to fill in the blank space with a word or phrase that makes it true. Usually the missing information is found in lecture notes or in the textbook in the form of main ideas and supporting details. Reviewing recall questions is an excellent way to prepare for fill-in type objective tests. Follow the strategy below to improve your grades on fill-in tests.

1. Read all of the directions carefully.

2. Read the first statement. If you know the missing information that will make the statement true, write the answer in the blank provided.

3. If you are not sure of the answer, skip this statement and go on to the next one. Sometimes the answers you need will be contained in other statements.

4. After you have completed filling in all the blanks that you can, go back to the statement(s) you did not know and look for key words. This can help jar your memory to recall facts from your notes or textbook.

5. If you are not going to be penalized for wrong answer, do not leave any blanks empty. Always take a guess since partial credit may be given.

6. If a word bank containing all the possible answers is provided, don't forget to cross out each word after using it.

Exercise
Fill-In Tests

Directions: **The following statements include information about computers. Read each sentence and fill in each blank with the answer from the list of words in the box.**

modem	keyboard	mouse	CD Rom
ram	pixel	gigabyte	menu
printer	monitor	port	

1. Although it doesn't squeak, a _____ does move a cursor around.

2. If you want to surf the internet at a high speed you need a fast _____.

3. It may look like a T.V. screen but it is really a _____.

4. If you want a thousand bytes of memory get a _____.

5. After reading this _____, a waiter won't come up, but your programs will.

6. The part of the computer's memory available for work with programs and documents is known as _____.

7. An entire encyclopedia can be contained on one _____.

8. Typewriters and computers both have a _____.

9. A socket on the back panel of the computer where you can plug in a cable to connect another device is called a _____.

10. To get a hard copy of information, you will use your _____

Answers can be found in Appendix A

Strategy
Taking Multiple Choice Tests

Some people like multiple choice tests while others do not. Actually, multiple choice questions can be helpful to you because the correct answer is given in one of the choices. Multiple choice questions begin with a statement. You must then choose one correct answer from a number of choices. In most multiple choice questions, one choice is included that is obviously incorrect. Often, though, two choices seem possible, but you must choose the "best" answer. This is when following the strategies will help you the most.

Follow the strategy below to improve your chances for a good grade on multiple choice tests.

1. Read all directions.

2. Read the first question and attempt to predict an answer *before* reading the answer choices.

3. Read all answer choices and eliminate all impossible answers (actually cross them out with one line).

4. Choose the answer that makes the most sense to you. Make sure it answers the question and relates to the topic and details that you have been studying.

5. Negative questions, worded such as "which one is NOT a reason" or "all the following are included EXCEPT ... " seem difficult because it is easier to recall facts that are included in what you have read. Read each answer choice and decide if that fact was included. Eliminate those, and you should then be left with only one answer.

6. Guess if you are still unsure, unless you are penalized for guessing.

7. If you need to bubble in your responses on a separate answer sheet, be careful to record the right choice by the right number.

Exercise
Taking a Practice Multiple Choice Test

Directions: Circle the correct letter of the answer that best completes each statement.

1. The capital of the United States is:

    a. Argentina, S.A.   b. Butte, Montana   c. Austin, Texas   d. Washington, D.C.
    e. New York, N.Y.

2. The national anthem of the U.S. is:

    a. The Star Spangled Banner   b. American Pie   c. America the Beautiful
    d. Glory, Glory Hallelujah   e. Hail to the Chief

3. The head of the British monarchy is:

    a. the president   b. the prime minister   c. the king or queen   d. the Beatles
    e. none of the above

4. The part of the sentence that tells who or what the sentence is about is the:

    a. direct object   b. verb   c. subject   d. predicate
    e. noun

5. The clause that describes a noun or pronoun is:

    a. Santa Claus   b. adverbial clause   c. independent clause d. adjective clause
    e. subordinate clause

6. To find information about the gymnastic career of Mary Lou Retton, you should look in:

    a. an atlas   b. a science magazine c. a dictionary   d. a phone directory
    e. an encyclopedia

7. To find information about the baseball career of Babe Ruth you should look in an encyclopedia under:

    a. baseball   b. Babe   c. career   d. Ruth
    e   sports

8. All of the following are states EXCEPT:

    a. Oregon   b. Maine   c. Washington, D.C. d. New York
    e. Texas

Answers can be found in Appendix A

Exercise
Check What You Know About Taking Tests

I. Read the following statements and circle the letter of the best answer.

1. Memorization of specific information is necessary.
   a. matching   b. fill-ins   c. true/false   d. multiple choice   e. all of the above

2. More than one choice may appear to be true.
   a. matching   b. fill-ins   c true/false   d. multiple choice   e. all of the above

3. Beware of absolutes like "all" and "never."
   a. matching   b. fill-ins   c. true/false   d. multiple choice   e. all of the above

4. Answer the easier ones first.
   a. matching   b. fill-ins   c. true/false   d. multiple choice   e. all of the above

5. Work the column with less choices first.
   a. matching   b.fill-ins   c. true/false   d. multiple choice   e. all of the above

II. Read the statement and fill in the answer that best completes the statement.

6. Specific facts, such as _____, _____, _____, _____, and _____ are often found on objective tests.

7. The first step when taking a test is to _____.

8. In order for a statement to be true, the _____ sentence must be true.

9. A review of _____ _____ is a helpful way to study for objective tests.

10. There are _____ types of objective tests.

III. Write (T) if the statement is true or (F) if the statement is false for the following statements.

11.___ In matching, if both columns have the same number of choices, work the column with the explanations first.

12.___ Words like "some," "usually," and "probably" are always found in true statements.

13.___ The order of the information presented can determine whether the statement is true or false.

14.___ Multiple choice questions can be difficult because choices are often similar and tricky.

15.___ Always guess on fill-in tests.

IV. Match the word in column A to its explanation in column B.

A	B
___ 16. ringer	a. answer can include opinions
___ 17. objective	b. the extraneous example on a matching test
___ 18. subjective	c. rarely happens
___ 19. scantron	d. type of test given most often
___ 20. never	e. a separate answer sheet, usually multiple choice, that requires you to "bubble" in answers
	f. usually false on a True/False test

Answers can be found in Appendix A

Strategy

Taking Essay Tests

This strategy will help you to learn what teachers expect you to write when they use certain key words. You will earn the maximum points if you make sure that your essay answers the question. The following terms are usually included in the directions for essays:

Questions that include these words require you to write all the **relevant** information you know about the subject:

• **Describe**	• **Discuss**	• **Explain**	• **List**
• **Outline**	• **Prove**	• **Review**	• **State**

Questions that include these words require you to write **specific facts** in a **specific way**:

• **Compare**	Write about the likenesses *and* differences of the subjects. *Compare the presidencies of Ronald Reagan and Jimmy Carter.*
• **Contrast**	Write about the differences *only* between the subjects. *Contrast the writing styles of William Shakespeare and Judy Blume.*
• **Compare and Contrast**	Write about the likenesses *and* differences of the subjects. *Compare and contrast the benefits of private and public education.*
• **Define**	Write the meaning of the word or subject given.
• **Illustrate**	Give examples that would explain, almost draw a picture about the topic.
• **Diagram**	You do not need to write, but only to draw and carefully label charts, tables, time lines, etc.

Questions that include these words require you to write **your opinion** backed up by **facts**:

• **Criticize**	• **Evaluate**	• **Interpret**	• **Justify**

Strategy
How to Begin the Essay

Once you understand essay terms you are ready to organize your thoughts as to how to answer the question. This strategy will help you to form a pattern you can use every time you start an essay.

Directions:

1. Read the essay question.
   Example: Discuss ways, both positive and negative, that computers are affecting the world. Include a discussion of your own experiences with computers.

2. Write a brief outline of the main points you want to include.
   Example: 1- Positive: communication, information
   2- Negative: impersonal, time-consuming, expensive
   3- Personal: E-Mail, games, WWW

3. Reread the essay question and restate it. This will be your opening or lead sentence. This sentence should lead the reader to the details.

   To restate the question: First, find the subject of the sentence (What is affecting the world? Computers).
   Next, use that as the subject of your lead sentence.
   Example: Computers are affecting the world in both positive and negative ways.

4. Write the essay by following your lead sentence with the facts in your outline. Conclude the essay with a restatement of your lead sentence.

Exercise
How to Begin the Essay Test

Directions: Read the essay questions below and restate them as lead sentences for an essay. You don't need to know anything about the subject to do this exercise; you just need to use the information in the essay question to rewrite it into a statement.

EXAMPLE:

The question: *Evaluate the results of requiring all students to wear school uniforms.*

Your sentence: *I believe that requiring all students to wear uniforms in school has resulted in the students feeling more relaxed about how they look.*

1. The question: How are rap music and country music alike in the way they depict life?

   Your sentence: _____

   _____

2. The question: Discuss the various theories, such as a meteorite, disease, or climate change, as reasons why dinosaurs became extinct.

   Your sentence: _____

   _____

3. The question: Describe how advances in communication technology have affected your life.

   Your sentence: _____

   _____

4. The question: Do standardized achievement tests (such as the SAT) really test what students know?

   Your sentence: _____

   _____

Strategy

Taking Subjective Tests

Essay tests can be a terrific way for you to earn grade points. Why? Essays give you a chance to tell everything that you know and earn some points even when you can't recall every detail about the subject. If you are very familiar with the subject, the essay is your place to shine.

- Essay questions involve major themes and how the facts relate to them. Therefore, it is essential to understand main ideas and supporting details.

- One excellent tool in preparing for a subjective test is to use your previously written outline, mind map or combo notes and recall questions of the main ideas and supporting details from texts and class discussions. Your recall questions may even be your test questions.

- Essay tests require an answer of at least one paragraph length. You will usually be required to focus upon the main points and general concepts more than on details. However, details must be included in your essay to back up, illustrate, or prove your main points.

Directions:

1. **Read** all directions and questions carefully.

2. **Decide** how much time you will spend on each essay.

3. **Begin** with the essay easiest for you. It will allow you to relax, gain confidence and recall facts.

4. **Jot** pertinent ideas in the margins that you want to use in your essay. Number ideas in the order you plan to use them.

5. **Begin** each answer by restating the question as your lead sentence.

6. **Use** the information you wrote in the margins to write main ideas first. Then fill in supporting details: facts, names, etc.

7   **Leave** space between answers to go back and add information.

8. **Reread**. Did you answer the question?

9. **Answer** all questions. Write all you are sure of for partial credit.

10. **Be specific**; use relevant facts.

11. **Proofread** for grammar, punctuation, spelling and NEATNESS (it does count).

12. **Remember**: Concise, well-organized answers are favored by teachers (which translates into better grades for you!).

Exercise

Test Taking

Directions: **Review your highlighting notes and recall questions for *Pompeii* on pages 51 and 52 and *King Henry VIII* on pages 59 and 60. Use the information to write an essay that answers the following questions.**

1. Why is Pompeii considered to be one of the the most remarkable preservations of its time?

2. How did Henry VIII manage to change the course of religion in England?

Strategy

Making Old Tests Work for You

One of the most valuable study aids you have is a returned test. By analyzing your errors, you can learn from your mistakes and actually plan ways to score higher on future tests. Also, if information was important enough to be included on the test, it may show up again on your midterm or final exam. Sometimes teachers do not return tests or only review them briefly during class. In these cases, speak with your teacher to arrange a convenient time to meet in order to go over the test. Be sure to bring this book with you so that you can fill in the charts below.

1. Analyze the type of questions missed or the points deducted for each type of question.

	Type of question included on test?	Total points or # of questions included	Points or # of questions missed
matching			
true/false			
fill-ins			
multiple choice			
short answer			
essay			

Which type of questions did you miss the most?_____
Review the test-taking strategies for the type(s) of questions you missed.

2. Were the questions missed:
    _____ a. details (people, places, events, vocabulary)?
    _____ b. general (short answer or essay)?
    _____ c. thought or application questions with answers not specifically given in book?
To prepare for your next test, remember that detail questions require recall of facts. You must consistently review the information. When you study for short answer and essay tests, you must understand how the details relate to the major concepts. When you have test questions that require the application of facts to other situations, you must be able to recall the facts and then apply your knowledge to different situations.

3. Was this test prepared by _____ your teacher _____ the publisher _____ other?
    Is this typical of past tests given by the teacher? _____ If not, how was this different?

_____

_____

If the test is prepared by the publisher, also study section and chapter questions and reviews. If the test questions are similar to those from past tests, you will know what to probably expect on future tests.

4. Look at the first question missed on your returned test. Find the answer in your book.
   Was it already highlighted?_____ Was it in your notes? _____
   Was it a review question in the text?_____ Was it in your recall questions?_____
   Fill in the following chart using the above questions. Put "N" for each "No".

Question missed (number only)	Was it highlighted?	In your notes?	In review or recall questions?

If you have three or more N's in the column titled "Was it highlighted?", you should review "3 Sweeps or How to Really Read a Textbook." It takes much practice to highlight effectively. Keep working and your grades will improve! If you have three or more N's under "In your notes?", you should review the note-taking strategy for simple outlining, mind mapping or combo notes. You may want to compare your notes with the notes of a friend who is a really good notetaker. If you have three or more N's under "In review or recall questions?", review "Recall Questions." Don't forget to review your recall questions daily.

5. To study for this test, did you: _____ cram the night before? _____ study over several
   days? _____review recall questions daily? _____use special memory techniques?
   Which ones?_____
   To prepare for your next text, begin today! Read and highlight the information. Write recall questions. REVIEW NIGHTLY. Review memory techniques and use them.
   _____

6. Were there any surprises on this test? ____ Yes _____No If yes, explain:
   _____

7. Use the above information to list what you can do to better prepare for the next test in this
   class. Before the next test I plan to:.
   1._____
   2._____
   3._____
   4._____
   5._____
   If the test is returned to you, write the correct answers. You may see these questions again on your mid-term or final exam. Be sure to save your vocabulary cards, notes, and graded tests, filing them by subject and chapter.

Strategy

Studying for Mid-Terms and Final Exams

Mid-term and final exams are given to test your ability to organize, understand, and recall information that has been taught over a period of weeks or even months. Since these tests are usually given for more than one subject and at around the same time, it is easy to feel overloaded with studying. To help, you need a method of preparation that will allow you to accomplish as much as possible without wasting valuable time.

The good news is that since you have been highlighting, taking notes, writing and reviewing recall questions, and learning information for chapter tests, you are better prepared than you may think. Now it's time for you to put all of those strategies together and show how well you have really been able to learn. So, enter those tests with confidence!

I. Get a Head Start Two Weeks Before the Exam.

   A. Find out all that you can about the exam.

      1. In class, listen for the teacher's clues and signals as to which material might be included on the tests.

      2. What type format will the test be?

         a. If objective only, review and memorize important details.

         b. If subjective also, learn overall concepts, but memorize enough facts to back them up in an essay.

      3. Can you bring notes into the exam? (Find out any limits as to how many pages, etc.)

      4. Will any chapters or material not be included on the test? (Unless the teacher tells you exactly what won't be included, study every chapter and all material.)

   B. Start the preparation

      1. Get out your filed notes, old tests, etc., and organize them now.

      2. Make sure that all chapters have been highlighted and recall questions written.

      3. Make up a study schedule to follow for the next two weeks.

C. Organize your study session.
1. Follow the study schedule and pace yourself so that you can study a little each day.
   a. Divide the number of chapters or pages to cover by the number of days you have set aside to study.
   b. Study each subject for one-half hour before breaking and beginning the next.
2. As you review the textbook, also review the lecture notes and clues from the teacher.
3. Review old tests since the same questions (possibly worded differently) may show up again.
4. For each chapter, concentrate on highlighted material and recall questions. Also, read and answer end of chapter study questions.

D. Remember to use your strongest learning style and preferences.
1. Auditory learners may want to read the highlighted information aloud, or tape record recall questions that you can then listen to and answer later.
2. Visual learners may want to picture the look of a page or associations.
3. Kinesthetic learners may want to rewrite information (e.g.,brief summary outlines or charts).
4. Study during the times and in the environments that will help you focus best.

II. Cramming
A. If you have consistently followed the strategies from *Study Strategies Made Easy*, you should not have to cram. However, just in case ...

B. What is cramming and how can you use it?
1. Cramming is really stuffing as much information into your head as possible just before you'll need to use it, such as the night before or morning of a test!
2. Unfortunately, cramming only works for very brief periods and for very small amounts of information, so it is not an efficient study strategy.
3. If you find that you absolutely must cram, don't try to read and remember every bit of information from the chapters and notes. Rely upon your highlighted information, vocabulary, and recall questions. This will be the most important information, and you can cram it into your memory in the shortest amount of time.

III. Final Words About Final Exams.
Successful test takers relax before exams. They go to sleep early, wake up early to eat a nutritious breakfast, listen to some soothing music, and pump themselves up with confident attitudes. Take advice from the successful test takers and be a successful test taker yourself!

CHAPTER 8
HANDLING HOMEWORK

Students who enjoy doing homework say they like the feeling of accomplishment when a project or assignment is completed. Also, they like the challenge of learning and discovering new information while doing homework.

Homework is part of our educational tradition. If you have a difficult time with homework, this chapter will give you easy-to-use strategies for getting it done. We hope that after you finish this section, you'll become more aware of your homework habits and the strategies you can use to improve them.

The strategies included in this chapter are:

- **Homework – Ugh!**
- **Homework Habit Checklist**
- **Homework Hassles, Homework Helpers**
- **Doing Homework Pays Dividends**

Strategy

Homework—Ugh!

Homework, as annoying as it is for some people, has been a part of American school life for as long as most people can remember. Although most students don't really like doing homework, there are some important benefits to it, and that is why teachers usually assign it.

Take a minute to list every complaint you have about doing homework:

1. _____
2. _____
3. _____
4. _____
5. _____
6. _____
7. _____
8. _____
9. _____
10. _____

(Please feel free to use another paper if you need more space.)

Okay, now think of as many really good reasons as you can to explain how homework helps you learn. We've supplied three. Try to give us a few more.

1. Homework allows you to get a chance to practice a newly learned skill.

2. Homework allows you to check your understanding of a new skill and ask questions about anything you are unclear about before you are tested on it.

3. Homework allows you to build the habit of working independently to solve problems.

4. _____

5. _____

6. _____

7. _____

Homework Habits Checklist

Directions: Answer the questions below to become more aware of your homework habits.

1. When homework is assigned in class, how do you remember what to do?
   - a. I write it in an assignment book
   - b. I write it in one of my notebooks
   - c. I write it down on any available paper
   - d. I don't write it; I usually just remember it

2. Where do you usually do your homework?
   - a. in my room
   - b. in the kitchen, den, etc.
   - c. at the library
   - d. at school
   - e. at a friend's house
   - f. other_____

3. When do you usually do your homework?
   - a. usually shortly after school
   - b. after dinner or work
   - c. late, after an activity (T.V., phone calls, etc.)
   - d. in the morning before school
   - e. the next day in class

4. How much time do you usually spend on homework each day?
   - a. barely enough
   - b. enough to do a thorough job
   - c. more than enough
   - d. definitely not enough

5. When you have a big assignment which is due in a week or two, how do you usually break it up?
   - a. I don't plan it. I just do it all at once
   - b. I usually do a little each night
   - c. I procrastinate until the very end, then I do it
   - d. I do it immediately and get it out of the way

6. How would you describe your attitude about homework?
   - a. I think it's a waste of time
   - b. I don't like it, but I do it anyway
   - c. I don't mind it as long as I learn something
   - d. I actually enjoy homework

7. In which subject do you dislike getting homework the <u>most</u>? Why?

   _____

8. In which subject do you dislike getting homework the <u>least</u>? Why?

   _____

9. Put a check ✔ next to any of the strategies listed below which you think could help you do a better job with homework. If you already use the strategy, circle the ✔ you put in the blank space.

   _____ write all assignments in an assignment book
   _____ break long-term or large assignments into smaller parts and do them a little at a time
   _____ do homework in a distraction-free environment
   _____ start homework as soon as I can after school
   _____ start homework as soon as I can after dinner
   _____ start homework as soon as I can in the evening after I relax awhile
   _____ take breaks every so often while doing homework

Strategy

Homework Hassles, Homework Helpers

Even though there are some very good reasons why teachers give homework, we admit it can be a hassle, so we've come up with some ideas to help you "grin and bear it."

1. **When I get home from school, I can't remember which homework I am supposed to do.**
   Even if you think you will remember homework, use your assignment book to write down every assignment.

2. **Sometimes when I get home from school, I have forgotten the books I need in order to do the assignment.**
   Before you leave a class and before you leave school for the day, look at your assignment book to check that you have all the materials you will need to do homework.

3. **I don't always understand the work, so I can't understand the homework.**
   Before you leave a class, reread your assignment book to be sure you understand the assignment. If not, ask another student or the teacher to clarify it for you.

4. **Sometimes it seems like there's too much to do and I feel overwhelmed and can't get it all done.**
   Estimate how long you believe each assignment should take. Decide whether anything can be left until tomorrow. Then, prioritize with a to-do list. Reschedule non-homework activities to give yourself as much time as possible.

5. **I work too slowly or I lose concentration, so I don't always finish.**
   If you have trouble staying on task or work slowly, set a timer for 20 minutes. Work diligently during that time, then reward yourself with a mini-break. After about five minutes, return to work. If homework assignments contine to be too heavy, see if your teacher will modify the amount for you or give you more time to complete it.

6. **After I turn in an assignment, the teacher says it's not complete enough.**
   Find out from the teacher why you are being penalized. While doing your assignment, make sure that you have included all the necessary details and answered the question. Reread the question to check that your answer is complete.

7. **After I get to school, I can't find my work, even though I've done it.**
   Follow the plan for organizing your materials. Immediately put all your completed work into your bookbag.

Strategy
Doing Homework Pays Dividends

Directions: Answer the questions below to become more aware of the benefits of homework.

1. Why do teachers assign homework?

   _____

   _____

   _____

2. Why should you complete your homework by the time it is due?

   _____

   _____

   _____

3. Why do students who do their homework score better on tests?

   _____

   _____

   _____

4. What can the teacher learn by reviewing your homework?

   _____

   _____

   _____

5. Describe two homework assignments that really helped you learn something important.

   _____

   _____

   _____

   _____

CHAPTER 9
STRESS MANAGEMENT STRATEGIES

The way in which we react emotionally to circumstances can affect our performance in school. As any athlete will tell you, you have to be in top shape mentally as well as physically to perform at your best. Most athletes use psychological strategies to help them get mentally prepared and cope with stress to meet challenges.

We have included a few of these sports psychology strategies in *Study Strategies Made Easy* to help you keep in top mental shape, while you are performing in school. The strategies we will discuss are:

- **Keeping a Positive Attitude**
- **Staying Relaxed Under Stress**
- **Using Visualization to Relax**
- **Handling Test Anxiety**
- **Reaching Goals Through Affirmations**

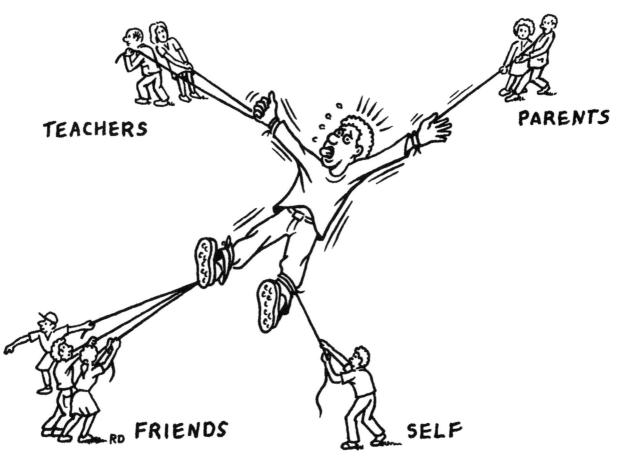

Strategy

Keeping a Positive Attitude

Life can either be seen as a bowl of cherries or a pile of pits, and whether you see things as an optimist or as a pessimist can make a big difference in your success in school. Positive thinkers usually face new challenges with energy and confidence. Unlike negative thinkers, they spend less time complaining about assignments, worrying about how they are going to get something done, and fearing bad grades. Therefore, they have a lot of mental energy available to be creative and productive.

Directions: **Answer these questions about yourself to see if you are a positive or negative thinker by checking "Yes" or "No."**

Yes	No	
_____	_____	1. I often enter a test situation thinking I am going to do well.
_____	_____	2. I usually start new assignments right away.
_____	_____	3. When I write reports I usually like the way they turn out
_____	_____	4. I am pretty optimistic about my grades on tests and papers.
_____	_____	5. I usually feel good about myself and about others.

If you answered "No" to most of these questions, you can probably use a good dose of positive thinking. Here's how you can begin to change your negative thoughts into positive ones.

✎ **Start by recognizing the types of negative thoughts you have.** We sometimes become so used to thinking one way that we don't ever recognize what we are doing. On the next page keep the diary for two days of all the negative thoughts you have. Thoughts like, "Oh my gosh, I'm going to fail this test" or "I'll never be able to study for math" or "I look awful today" count as negative thoughts.

✎ **Use your list of negative thoughts and write the opposite, positive thought.** In other words, change the negative thought into a positive thought. Repeat the positive thought aloud five times and then say it to yourself five times.

✎ **Practice thinking positive.** Once you've figured out what negative thoughts trouble you the most; turn them into positive thoughts. For many people, negative thinking has become a bad habit. Habits get stronger when we rehearse them or repeat them over and over. They get weaker when we do them less or stop them altogether. By catching ourselves thinking negatively, replacing negative thoughts with positive ones, and repeating those positive thoughts over and over, we can replace a negative thinking habit with a positive thinking habit.

✎ **Change your thoughts to positive ones.** If you find yourself dwelling on negative thoughts too much, stop thinking and change your thoughts to something else much as you would change the station on the radio if you didn't like the song. Remember, you have control of how you think. Negative thinking never does anyone any good, while positive thinking does wonders. You'll feel better, and you'll perform better.

Exercise
Reverse, Don't Rehearse Negative Thinking

Directions: Keep a diary of your thoughts for the next two days. Write down any negative thoughts that come to mind; then write down a positive thought to replace it.

NEG _____

POS _____

NEG _____

POS _____

NEG _____

POS _____

NEG _____

POS _____

NEG _____

POS _____

NEG _____

POS _____

Remember, to some extent, negative thinking is like a bad habit. The more you do it the stronger the habit becomes. Reverse, don't rehearse negative thinking. Recite the positive thoughts you've written to yourself and use them to replace negative thoughts in the future.

Strategy

Staying Relaxed under Stress

When faced with a stressor, our body's autonomic nervous system kicks into action. Our heart beats faster sending more blood to our muscles, brain, and organ systems, making them better prepared to deal with the stress. We are ready to protect ourselves from the stressor, either by fight or flight. Stress can lead to good things as well as bad things. For instance, stress over grades motivates us to study and be prepared. However, stress can also be very damaging. Excessive stress can create physical problems, can interfere with our ability to concentrate or to sleep well at night, and can cause us to be moody or irritable.

Directions: Do you have any of the following stress indicators? Check the ones you get when you feel tense.

_____ headaches	_____ nervousness	_____ overly sensitive
_____ stomach aches	_____ restlessness	_____ change in appetite
_____ muscle tension	_____ irritable mood	_____ poor concentration
_____ difficulty sleeping	_____ excessive worrying	_____ angry outbursts

When stress gets out of hand and you begin to show signs of physical, social, or emotional difficulties, you will need to learn to cope with it another way. Here are a few ways people have found to cope with stress:

- **Work out.** Get some physical exercise. Walking, jogging, working out in some way can take your mind off a problem and can help your body recharge.

- **Tell somebody how you feel.** Talking about your feelings with someone who is supportive and trustworthy can help you feel better.

- **Take a break from the pressure**. If you are working too hard at school, take some time off. If there are too many demands on your time, i.e. job and school work, take a look at your schedule and see if you can make some changes to make life a little easier.

- **Analyze your thinking**. Are you creating stress by negative thinking? Perhaps you can follow the steps in the preceeding strategy to change negative thoughts into positive ones.

Strategy

Using Visualization to Relax

Visualization is an excellent method to help you achieve relaxation. By visualizing ourselves in a restful, relaxing environment, we can remove negative thoughts from our minds and experience a calm feeling throughout our bodies. This exercise will help you focus on a scene which many people find relaxing. To do this exercise, find a comfortable, quiet place which is free of distractions.

Imagine yourself taking a walk along a fresh, clear stream of water in a beautiful valley surrounded by mountains. You stop to relax on a grassy area near the stream. You find the perfect spot to rest and you lie down and close your eyes. Imagine yourself lying there. Calm, peaceful, and relaxed. Your breathing becomes easy, your body begins to feel calm, and your mind becomes quiet. You can hear the sound of birds chirping in the distance and the water running across the rocks in the stream. You can smell the fresh scent of the grass and flowers and feel the gentle breezes of the air around you. The sun warms your body and you feel quiet and relaxed.

As you lie there you repeat these three phrases to yourself:

I feel calm and relaxed.
My mind is at ease.
My body is relaxed.

I feel calm and relaxed.
My mind is at ease.
My body is relaxed.

I feel calm and relaxed.
My mind is at ease.
My body is relaxed.

Continue with this exercise for ten minutes, occasionally repeating the relaxation phrases to yourself and visualizing the comfortable scene described above.

At other times, try to visualize different scenes that you find relaxing. Some ideas are:
- **floating in a pool**
- **floating on a cloud**
- **sitting on a golf course**
- **lying on the beach**
- **lying in bed at home**

Strategy
Handling Test Anxiety

Many people get nervous before a test. It is normal to worry in test situations. However, if your worrying and nervousness are interfering with your ability to concentrate and think straight, you may be suffering from test anxiety.

Some causes of test anxiety may be: a lack of confidence, overconcern about grades and doing well, pressure from others, failure to do well on tests in the past. If on the days you take tests, your palms sweat, your nerves get rattled, and your stomach is doing flips ... you may be suffering from test anxiety.

Here's the good news! Test anxiety can be helped. Here's how.

1. **Be prepared for tests by reviewing information well in advance.** Waiting until the last minute to study will only make you more nervous.

2. **Don't overemphasize the importance of any test.** For example, don't say things like this to yourself: "If I don't pass this test I will fail the course and my life will be ruined." Instead, say things like this to yourself: "This is only one of many tests I'll take. I will stay calm and do the best I can."

3. **Get a good night's sleep the night before the test.** Eat well on the day of the test.

4. **Use your visualization strategy to relax the night before and on the day of the test.** It is best to first visualize yourself in a relaxing situation and then repeat the calming phrases to yourself found on the previous page.

5. **Do the exercise on the next page to help you relax in a test situation.**

Exercise

Desensitize Yourself to Test Anxiety

Directions: **You can learn to become more relaxed before or during a test by using a process psychologists call systematic desensitization. This is really a simple process in which you relax while visualizing different test-taking scenes which cause nervousness. Follow these steps:**

Look at the list of test-taking scenes that sometimes make students nervous:

1. thinking the night before about tomorrow's test

2. waking up the morning of the test and thinking about it

3. walking to school on the day of the test

4. going into the classroom where you will take the test

5. sitting at your desk with the test in front of you

6. reading the test at your desk and answering the questions

(Add situations of your own to this list if you like)

7. _____

8. _____

9. _____

10. _____

Now follow these steps:

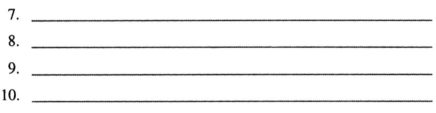 Start your desensitization at home by finding a comfortable place to relax.

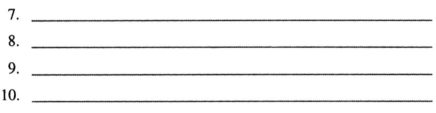 Next, visualize a calm, relaxing scene such as the one in the visualization strategy (lying by a stream, etc.).

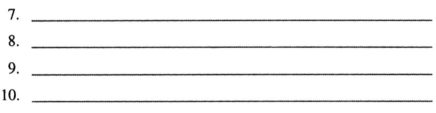 Once you've begun to relax, switch your visual image to the test-taking scene at the top of the list. If picturing this scene makes you feel tense, stop and switch to the relaxing scene.

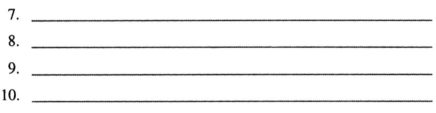 After you've relaxed again, switch back to the test-taking scene. Associate the test scene with feeling relaxed. If picturing this scene makes you feel tense, stop and switch again to the relaxing scene.

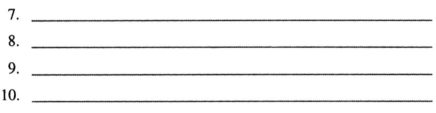 Once you are able to imagine a test-taking scene and can stay relaxed, move on to the next test-taking scene and try to stay relaxed again.

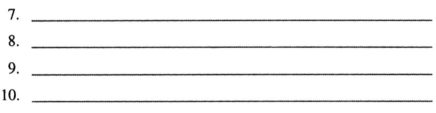 Continue until you make your way through all the test-taking scenes on your list. Keep in mind that it may take two or more sessions to get you through the whole list.

Strategy

Reaching Goals through Affirmations

Affirmations are positive statements we recite to ourselves to help us stay focused on important goals. Psychologists believe that we are more likely to reach our goals if we consistently focus on them.

For example, if you wanted to become more outgoing and friendly towards others, you might recite the following affirmation as a reminder: "I will say hello to others and speak to them in a friendly way." If you wanted to focus on paying better attention in class, you might recite the following affirmation: "I can listen closely to the teacher."

Affirmations allow us to focus on a specific goal. They work best when we get relaxed and repeat them to ourselves over and over. Through frequent repetition, the goal embedded in the affirmation is given a high priority throughout the days, weeks, or months that you recite the affirmation.

Remember, affirmations are **positive** statements about yourself, not negative ones.

Directions:
1. Use the spaces below to write three to five affirmations for yourself.

2. Take 1-3 minutes each day for about a week, close your eyes, and recite one or two of the affirmations written below to yourself.

3. After one week, pick another one or two affirmations and recite those to yourself 1-3 minutes per day for another week.

1. _____

2. _____

3. _____

4. _____

5. _____

NOW THAT WE'VE FINISHED . . .
A CHECKLIST OF STUDY STRATEGIES

Now that you have finished *Study Strategies Made Easy*, you can re-evaluate your study skills. Answer the questions below to evaluate your study strengths and weaknesses. Read each question. If you *almost* always do what is asked, write "Yes"; *almost never* do what is asked, write "No"; *sometimes* do what is asked, write "S". Then, write the number of your **yes** answers in the score box below. How are *your* present study skills rated, now?

ORGANIZATION

_____ 1. Do I have all of the supplies I need for school?

_____ 2. Do I keep my notebooks and materials organized so that I can easily find what I need?

_____ 3. Do I keep a schedule of study times and activities?

_____ 4. Do I write my assignments in an assignment notebook?

_____ 5. Do I have an organized plan for the order I do my assignments?

_____ 6. Do I complete and turn in my assignments on time?

_____ 7. Do I keep track of my grades on a weekly basis?

_____ 8. Do I keep and follow a written plan to complete long-term assignments?

LEARNING STYLE

_____ 9. Do I use my best style of learning when I study?

_____ 10. Do I understand where, when, and how I study best?

COMMUNICATION

_____ 11. Do my teachers usually see my behavior in the classroom in a positive way?

_____ 12. Do I usually know what each teacher expects of me?

_____ 13. Do I effectively talk to my teachers when I need help?

_____ 14. Do I discuss school-related problems I might have with my teachers?

_____ 15. Do I communicate well with other students and show respect for them?

READING COMPREHENSION

_____ 16. Can I identify topics, main ideas, and supporting details in a reading selection?

_____ 17. Do I understand without having to reread, what I am reading in my textbooks?

_____ 18. Can I summarize what I read in my own words?

_____ 19. Do I use signal words to help me identify important information in my textbooks?

_____ 20. Do I preview the textbook chapters?

_____ 21. Do I consistently read my textbook?

_____ 22. Do I have a successful method to learn new vocabulary and remember it during and after a test?

NOTE-TAKING

_____ 23. Do I take notes from lectures?

_____ 24. Do I get the important points from my teachers' lectures?

_____ 25. Do I use different ways to take accurate notes?

_____ 26. Do I use abbreviations for note-taking?

_____ 27. Do I turn my notes into study sheets?

_____ 28. Do I combine information from the textbook with my lecture notes?

_____ 29. Do I review my notes over a period of time?

MEMORIZATION

_____ 30. Do I know different ways to memorize beside reading information over and over?

_____ 31. Do I use different ways to memorize information?

_____ 32. When I take tests do I remember most of the facts I tried to memorize?

TEST-TAKING

_____ 33. While taking a test, do I very carefully follow directions?

_____ 34. Do I use appropriate strategies for taking different kinds of tests?

_____ 35. Do I keep old tests to use at a later time?

_____ 36. Do I analyze my errors from old tests to determine a pattern?

_____ 37. Do I effectively prepare for mid-terms and final exams?

_____ 38. Am I satisfied with my study habits?

_____ 39. Am I pleased with my grades?

DOING HOMEWORK

_____ 40. Do I use an assignment book?

_____ 41. Do I do homework in an environment that allows me to concentrate?

_____ 42. Do I spend enough time on homework to do a thorough job?

_____ 43. Do I complete homework by the time it is due?

STRESS MANAGEMENT

_____ 44. Am I confident that I can do well in school?

_____ 45. Do I have a positive, optimistic outlook about my schoolwork?

_____ 46. Do I feel as relaxed as most other students do about schoolwork and tests?

_____ 47. Do I know strategies to help me reduce stress and relax?

HIGHLIGHT YOUR RATING:		
42-47	YES = Superior Study Habits	SCORE: _____
36-41	YES = Good Study Habits	
29-35	YES = Average Study Habits	
below 28	YES = Needs Improvement	

Compare the score you received this time with your earlier score. Determine which strategies you are using more now as a result of this program. Do the evaluation exercise on the following page and you'll have a plan to increase your skills as you increase your success!

Exercise

Evaluating How *Study Strategies Made Easy* Worked for You

Directions: **Now that you know the stratagies for school success, complete this exercise to think about the changes that have taken place in your academic life and how you can utilize these strategies to become an even better student.**

1. Are you using the strategies in school? _____ Yes   _____ No
   Have you seen an improvement in your grades? _____ Yes   _____ No

2. Which strategies have helped you the most? How?

   _____

   _____

   _____

   _____

3. What strategies do you plan to use in the future?

   _____

   _____

   _____

   _____

4. Please write any additional comments below.

   _____

   _____

   _____

   _____

   _____

   _____

   _____

   _____

   _____

   _____

   _____

   _____

117

Appendix A
Answer Key

Page 41 — Finding Signals in Reading Selections

Hunters and Gatherers

(All) people of long ago had to get food and shelter just as we do (today) (However,) while we go to the store to buy our food, ancient populations had to rely upon the land.

(One) way that people got their food was to walk around the area picking what grew wild on trees and bushes, (such as) nuts and berries. (Another) way was to eat any plants or roots that could be dug up. (Both) of these methods are called gathering.

While gathering could supply vegetables, nuts and some fruits, humans (also) needed to eat meat. (Therefore) the cavemen learned to hunt (or) find and kill animals such as deer or rabbits.

(Because) most cavemen got their food by using both methods, they are now known as hunters and gatherers. This was their way of life, (or) culture. When people develop a culture, they must (also) devise the tools to keep that culture going. (For example,) early people invented tools that allowed them to dig up plants more easily, and weapons that allowed them to kill more effectively. (As a result) of their inventiveness, the early human populations survived and spread their culture throughout our world.

Page 47 — Using the 3 Sweeps Strategy in Reading

1. A comet is a nebular body that revolves around the sun.
2. Comets are made of ice and earth-like dust.
3. Because he found that comets were father away from Earth than the moon, people know comets weren't Earth's property.
4. Comets travel in an elongated orbit that is not random. This predictable path makes tracking comets easier.
5. Halley discovered that what looked to be several comets was actually one
6. We see the tail because it points closer to Earth.
7. One tail is made of gas or plasma. The other tail is made of dust and is curved and hazy.
8. The Tunguska River area in Siberia was hit by a comet which damaged miles of trees.

Page 51 — Simple Outlining Exercise

Title
Pompeii, the City Left Asleep for 1500 Years

I. Heading/Topic
    Eruption
   A.   Main idea
         Citizens unaware of potential for disaster
         1. Supporting detail
            Built upon the hardened lava from past
            volcanic eruption of Mt. Vesuvius, Italy
         2. Supporting detail
            Built mansions, traded + enjoyed lives
   B.   Main idea
         79 A.D. Mt. Vesuvius erupts
         1. Supporting detail
             Loud explosion
         2. Supporting detail
            Lava cascaded down onto homes
         3. Supporting detail
            Ash + pumice stone covered city
         4. Supporting detail
            Electrical storm that blocked out daylight
         5. Supporting detail
            Gaseous fumes killed remaining life.
         6. Supporting detail
            Rain hardens lava + buries city under
            eighteen feet crust.

II. Heading/Topic
     Discovery
   A.   Main idea
         Preservation most remarkable of its time
         1. Supporting detail
            Hermetically sealed > 1500 years
         2. Supporting detail
            Remains of 2000 people near-perfect
            condition.
   B.   Main idea
         Evidence found that people were
            surprised by eruption
         1. Supporting detail
            Food found

a) subdetail
   eggs unbroken
b) subdetail
   wine still drinkable
c) subdetail
   food on table uneaten
2. Supporting detail
   People in stages of action
   a) subdetail
      mother & daughter in embrace
   b) subdetail
      man defending gold

III. Heading/Topic
     City Now Alive
   A.   Main idea
         Pompei is bustling city
         1. Supporting detail
            3/5 ruins excavated
         2. Supporting detail
            Millions of visitors come
   B.   Main idea
         Dis wouldn't go uncovered again
         1. Supporting detail
            People now live on Mt. Vesuvious again
         2. Supporting detail
            Aware another eruption could happen

121

Page 57 — Mind Mapping the Brain

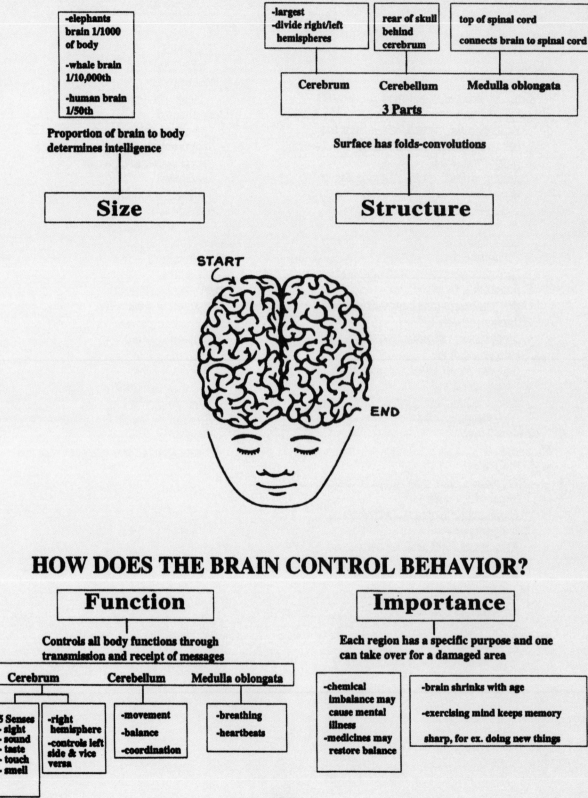

-elephants brain 1/1000 of body

-whale brain 1/10,000th

-human brain 1/50th

Proportion of brain to body determines intelligence

Size

-largest
-divide right/left hemispheres

rear of skull behind cerebrum

top of spinal cord

connects brain to spinal cord

Cerebrum   Cerebellum   Medulla oblongata

3 Parts

Surface has folds-convolutions

Structure

START

END

HOW DOES THE BRAIN CONTROL BEHAVIOR?

Function

Controls all body functions through transmission and receipt of messages

Cerebrum   Cerebellum   Medulla oblongata

5 Senses
- sight
- sound
- taste
- touch
- smell

-right hemisphere
-controls left side & vice versa

-movement
-balance
-coordination

-breathing
-heartbeats

Importance

Each region has a specific purpose and one can take over for a damaged area

-chemical imbalance may cause mental illness
-medicines may restore balance

-brain shrinks with age

-exercising mind keeps memory

sharp, for ex. doing new things

Page 60 — Taking Combo Notes Henry VIII

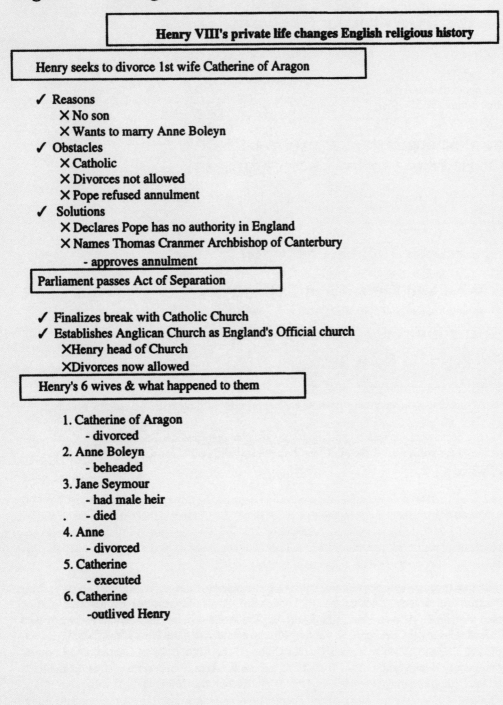

> **Henry VIII's private life changes English religious history**

Henry seeks to divorce 1st wife Catherine of Aragon

- ✓ Reasons
    - ✗ No son
    - ✗ Wants to marry Anne Boleyn
- ✓ Obstacles
    - ✗ Catholic
    - ✗ Divorces not allowed
    - ✗ Pope refused annulment
- ✓ Solutions
    - ✗ Declares Pope has no authority in England
    - ✗ Names Thomas Cranmer Archbishop of Canterbury
        - approves annulment

Parliament passes Act of Separation

- ✓ Finalizes break with Catholic Church
- ✓ Establishes Anglican Church as England's Official church
    - ✗ Henry head of Church
    - ✗ Divorces now allowed

Henry's 6 wives & what happened to them

1. Catherine of Aragon
    - divorced
2. Anne Boleyn
    - beheaded
3. Jane Seymour
    - had male heir
    . - died
4. Anne
    - divorced
5. Catherine
    - executed
6. Catherine
    - outlived Henry

Page 63 — Writing Recall Questions   1.D, 2.E, 3.B, 4.C, 5.F, 6.B, 7.A, 8.B, 9.F, 10.D

Pages 64 and 65 — Recall Questions for Note-taking
Who was Norman Cousins?
What happened to him?   ③
How did it affect him?
What were Cousins' beliefs about disease?   ③
What did Cousins do to help himself?   ③
What were results?   ⑥

Page 85 — Taking Matching Tests   1. D 2. G 3. A 4. F 5. E 6. C

Page 87 — True-False Tests   1 F, 2.T, 3.F, 4.F, 5.F, 6.T, 7.F, 8.F. 9.T

Page 89 — Fill-In Tests   1. mouse 2. modem 3. monitor 4. gigabyte 5. menu 6. ram

7. CD Rom 8. keyboard 9. port 10. printer

Page 91 — Taking a Practice Multiple Choice Test
1. d 2. a. 3. c. 4. c. 5. d. 6. e. 7. d. 8. c

Page 92 — Check What You Know About Taking Tests
1. e 2. d 3. c 4. e 5. a 6. definitions, dates, people, places, events 7. read directions 8. entire

9. recall questions 10. four 11. T 12. F 13. T 14. T 15. F 16. b 17. d 18. a 19. e 20. f

Page 95 — How to Begin the Essay Test

1. There are many ways that rap and country music treat life similarly.
2. Scientists have theorized that dinosaurs may have become extinct because of meteorites, diseases, or drastic climate changes.
3. My life has become better because of the new technological advances in communication.
4. Although achievement tests are widely used, they definitely do not test all I really know.

Page 97 — Test-Taking

1. Pompeii is considered to be a remarkable example of preservation because the city had been hermetically sealed for 1500 years. The excavations revealed intact remains of 2000 people. Furthermore, there was evidence of how surprised the citizens were. For example, eggs lay on tables unbroken and wine was still drinkable. Even people were found in the middle of an action, such as the mother and her daughter hugging or the man still defending his gold. For all these reaasons, Pompeii was preserved in unbelievable condition.

2. Henry VIII changed England's religious history almost entirely due to his own desires. When Henry became king in 1509, he married Catherine of Aragon. Because she didn't have a son and also because he was interested in Anne Boleyn, Henry wanted a divorce. At that time Catholicism was England's official religion and divorce wasn't allowed. Henry VIII took steps to get the divorce he wanted. First he declared that the Pope of the Catholic church no longer had authority in England. Then he named Thomas Cranmer The Archbishop of Canterbury. Cranmer granted Henry an annulment. Henry then pushed Parliament to pass the Acts of Separation. This act finalized England's break from the Catholic church and established the Anglican church as England's official church. Since the new Church of England had the king as its head and did permit divorce, Henry got all he wanted and the future of England was Anglican, not Roman Catholic. This is still true today.

Appendix B
Forms

Weekly Schedule Sheet

Get it Done Today To-Do List

Grade Chart

Goal-Setting Sheet for Long-Term Research Project

Understanding Teachers' Expectations

Accommodation Request Form

Making Old Tests Work for You

WEEKLY SCHEDULE SHEET

WEEK OF _____

TIME	MONDAY	TUESDAY	WEDNESDAY	THURSDAY	FRIDAY	SATURDAY	SUNDAY
4:00 - 5:00 or earlier							
5:00 - 5:30							
5:30 - 6:00							
6:00 - 6:30							
6:30 - 7:00							
7:00 - 7:30							
7:30 - 8:00							
8:00 - 8:30							
8:30 - 9:00							
9:00 - 9:30							
9:30 - 10:00							
10:00 - 10:30 or after							
AVAILABLE TIME / TIME USED FOR STUDY							

GET IT DONE TODAY

Date _____

Priority	Assignment	Date Due	Completed
_____	_____		☐
_____	_____		☐
_____	_____		☐
_____	_____		☐
_____	_____		☐
_____	_____		☐
_____	_____		☐
_____	_____		☐
_____	_____		☐
_____	_____		☐
_____	_____		☐

GRADE CHART

Quarter 1 2 3 4 _____
Beginning date _____

KEY:
T = test   Q = quiz
HW = homework
P = project

COURSE	WEEK 1	2	3	4	5	6	7	8	9	Report Card Grade
Grade I want___										
Grade I want___										
Grade I want___										
Grade I want___										
Grade I want___										
Grade I want___										
Grade I want___										

Goal-Setting Form for a Long-Term Research Project

REQUIREMENTS:

Assignment: _____

__ written; # of pages or words: _____

____ oral; amount of time ____

Format requirements: _____

_____

Other requirements: _____

_____

DATE DUE: _____

TARGET GRADE: ____

THE PRE-WRITE	Due by Date	Doing ✔ Done ✗

STEP 1: TENTATIVE TOPICS

_____

_____

STEP 2: PRELIMINARY RESEARCH

STEP 3: SELECT TOPIC

_____

STEP 4: COLLECT SOURCES

STEP 5: NARROW TOPIC

STEP 6: BRAINSTORM

_____

_____

_____

STEP 7: THESIS STATEMENT

_____

_____

THE FIRST WRITE

STEP 8: PRIORITIZE _____ _____
    A. _____
    B. _____
    C. _____

STEP 9: ROUGH OUTLINE _____ _____
    I. _____
    II. _____
    III. _____
    IV. _____
    V. _____

STEP 10: NOTE CARDS _____ _____

STEP 11: SORT CARDS _____ _____

STEP 12: ROUGH DRAFT _____ _____

THE HOME STRETCH

STEP 13: REVISE _____ _____

STEP 14: REWRITE _____ _____

STEP 15: EDIT _____ _____

STEP 16: FINAL COPY _____ _____

Strategy
Understanding Teachers' Expectations

The purpose of this strategy is to help you better understand how your teachers teach, what they emphasize, and from where test information is taken. This will allow you to predict what teachers expect of you.

Directions: **Under the column "Teacher or Class" write each of your teacher's or class names and as you go down the list check the space that best describes how teachers teach and test.**

TEACHER OR CLASS

How Information is Presented

1. Information written on chalkboard or overhead

2. Information presented in lecture and students take notes

Homework Assignments

3. Assigned for practice only and no grade is given

4. Assigned and graded

5. Checked to see if done

Questons on Tests Come From

6. Textbook chapters

7. Textbook questions

8. Teacher's lectures

9. Information found in outside sources

	/	/	/	/	/
1.	__	__	__	__	__
2.	__	__	__	__	__
3.	__	__	__	__	__
4.	__	__	__	__	__
5.	__	__	__	__	__
6.	__	__	__	__	__
7.	__	__	__	__	__
8.	__	__	__	__	__
9.	__	__	__	__	__

TEACHER OR CLASS

How Teachers Teach and Test

	/	/	/	/	/
10. Worksheets/packets	10. ___	___	___	___	___
11. Films/Labs	11. ___	___	___	___	___

Test Preparation

12. No review given	12. ___	___	___	___	___
13. Study sheets handed out	13. ___	___	___	___	___
14. Review is done orally in class	14. ___	___	___	___	___

Types of Tests Given

15. Multiple Choice	15. ___	___	___	___	___
16. True/False	16. ___	___	___	___	___
17. Matching	17. ___	___	___	___	___
18. Fill-ins	18. ___	___	___	___	___
19. Essays	19. ___	___	___	___	___
20. Tests vary	20. ___	___	___	___	___
21. Tests written by publisher	21. ___	___	___	___	___
22. Tests written by teacher	22. ___	___	___	___	___

By reading this chart you can "read your teacher" and match what and how you study to each teacher's unique needs. For instance,

- If the teacher lectures, use your notes to study asthe information from your notes is important.
- If homework is assigned and graded, do it well in order to add points to your grade.
- If you know from where teachers get their test questions, concentrate more on those materials.
- If a teacher doesn't review, you will need to review on your own. Pay close attenton in class, because daily lessons may include hints. If a teacher does review, study on your own anyway, but use the teacher's review to narrow down your final studying.

Accommodation Request Form

Dear _____,   Date: _____
      Teacher

Although I am trying to follow the study strategies to do well in your class, I still seem to be having some difficulty. On this sheet, I have checked the areas in which I have trouble and the classroom accommodations that might help me improve. Please check any problem areas that you have observed and any classroom accommodations you think might help me. Then, I would like to meet with you to discuss solutions that we both agree would help me improve. Thank you for your cooperation and help.

_____
Your Name

TCHR STDT TROUBLE WITH ORGANIZATION

- ❑ ❑ encourage student to use a calendar or planner
- ❑ ❑ write assignments on chalkboard
- ❑ ❑ allow ample time to copy assignments
- ❑ ❑ give reminders when assignments are due
- ❑ ❑ encourage student to purchase second set of books
- ❑ ❑ color code book covers and notebooks
- ❑ ❑ encourage use of pocket folders for filing papers
- ❑ ❑ break down large assignments into smaller parts

TCHR STDT TROUBLE COMPLETING ASSIGNMENTS

- ❑ ❑ use a written contract or work agreement
- ❑ ❑ use a weekly assignment/grade progress report
- ❑ ❑ be flexible on late work turned in
- ❑ ❑ mail home assignments for a week or two
- ❑ ❑ provide copy of class syllabus
- ❑ ❑ give immediate feedback on work turned in and test grades
- ❑ ❑ meet with student for feedback and direction
- ❑ ❑ check to see if student understands work assigned
- ❑ ❑ reduce homework assignment as long as student shows mastery

TCHR STDT TROUBLE WITH TEST TAKING

- ❑ ❑ allow extra time
- ❑ ❑ test in a distraction-free area
- ❑ ❑ allow breaks on long tests

TCHR STDT TROUBLE TAKING NOTES

- ❑ ❑ teacher provides outlines for student to fill in
- ❑ ❑ teacher provides copy of own notes
- ❑ ❑ share other student's notes
- ❑ ❑ use tape recorder for missing information

TCHR STDT TROUBLE PAYING ATTENTION

- ❑ ❑ involve student in class discussions
- ❑ ❑ seat student away from distractions
- ❑ ❑ cue student when directions are given
- ❑ ❑ simplify and repeat complex directions

TCHR STDT TROUBLE WITH BEHAVIOR

- ❑ ❑ determine reasons for behavior difficulties by meeting with student, parent, etc.
- ❑ ❑ post clear rules in classroom
- ❑ ❑ seat away from friends
- ❑ ❑ write a behavior contract
- ❑ ❑ develop a plan with student to help improve

TCHR STDT TROUBLE WITH HANDWRITING AND/OR SPELLING

- ❑ ❑ allow printing instead of cursive
- ❑ ❑ encourage use of typewriter or word processor
- ❑ ❑ allow copying of other student's notes
- ❑ ❑ reduce length of long written assignments
- ❑ ❑ reduce emphasis on neat handwriting/spelling
- ❑ ❑ encourage use of spell check systems

OTHER AREAS OF TROUBLE

_____

_____

Strategy

Making Old Tests Work for You

One of the most valuable study aids you have is a returned test. By analyzing your errors, you can learn from your mistakes and actually plan ways to score higher on future tests. Also, if information was important enough to be included on the test, it may show up again on your midterm or final exam. Sometimes teachers do not return tests or only review them briefly during class. In these cases, speak with your teacher to arrange a convenient time to meet in order to go over the test. Be sure to bring this book with you so that you can fill in the charts below.

1. Analyze the type of questions missed or the points deducted for each type of question.

	Type of question included on test?	Total points or # of questions included	Points or # of questions missed
matching			
true/false			
fill-ins			
multiple choice			
short answer			
essay			

Which type of questions did you miss the most?_____
Review the test-taking strategies for the type(s) of questions you missed.

2. Were the questions missed:
_____ a. details (people, places, events, vocabulary)?
_____ b. general (short answer or essay)?
_____ c. thought or application questions with answers not specifically given in book?
To prepare for your next test, remember that detail questions require recall of facts. You must consistently review the information. When you study for short answer and essay tests you must understand how the details relate to the major concepts. When you have test questions that require the application of facts to other situations, you must be able to recall the facts and then apply your knowledge to different situations.

3. Was this test prepared by _____ your teacher _____the publisher _____ other?
Is this typical of past tests given by the teacher? _____ If not, how was this different?

_____

_____

If the test is prepared by the publisher, also study section and chapter questions and reviews. If the test questions are similar to those from past tests, you will know what to probably expect on future tests.

4. Look at the first question missed on your returned test. Find the answer in your book.
Was it already highlighted?_____ Was it in your notes? _____
Was it a review question in the text?_____ Was it in your recall questions?_____
Fill in the following chart using the above questions. Put "N" for each "No".

Question missed (number only)	Was it highlighted?	In your notes?	In review or recall questions?

If you have three or more N's in the column titled "Was it highlighted?", you should review "3 Sweeps or How to Really Read a Textbook." It takes much practice to highlight effectively. Keep working and your grades will improve! If you have three or more N's under "In your notes?", you should review the note-taking strategy for simple outlining, mind mapping or combo notes. You may want to compare your notes with a friends' who is a really good notetaker. If you have three or more N's under "In review or recall questions?", review "Recall Questions." Don't forget to review your recall questions daily.

5. To study for this test, did you: _____ cram the night before? _____ study over several days? _____review recall questions daily? _____use special memory techniques? Which ones?_____
To prepare for your next text, begin today! Read and highlight the information. Write recall questions. REVIEW NIGHTLY. Review memory techniques and use them.
_____

6. Were there any surprises on this test? _____ Yes _____No If yes, explain:
_____

7. Use the above information to list what you can do to better prepare for the next test in this class. Before the next test I plan to:.
1._____
2._____
3._____
4._____
5._____

If the test is returned to you, write the correct answers. You may see these questions again on your mid-term or final exam. Be sure to save your vocabulary cards, notes, and graded tests, filing them by subject and chapter.

Appendix C
Lesson Plans for Instructors

LESSON PLANS FOR INSTRUCTORS

Study Strategies Made Easy is designed with the student and you, the instructor (teacher or parent), in mind. In this section of the book you will find a chapter-by-chapter explanation of the different strategies and exercises we've included in the text. While the *Study Strategies Made Easy* program was written to be completed by middle school and high school students with as little need for instructor assistance as possible, the lesson plans and suggestions that follow provide ideas for presenting the strategies. We know this is a valuable program and want it to be enjoyable for you and your students.

BEFORE YOU BEGIN

The Checklist of Study Strategies is a pre-test which allows students to discover for themselves the study strategies they presently use. The forty-seven items in the checklist are grouped within nine broad skill areas: ORGANIZATION, LEARNING STYLES, COMMUNICATION, READING COMPREHENSION, NOTE TAKING, MEMORIZATION, TEST TAKING, DOING HOMEWORK, and STRESS MANAGEMENT. These areas were selected for inclusion in the *Study Strategies Made Easy* program because they represent important skills which, if mastered, will help students succeed at the secondary school level. Each item in the checklist corresponds to a specific strategy covered in the text of the program.

Following a brief introduction to give the purpose of The Checklist of Study Strategies, ask the students to complete the checklist. Have students calculate their scores by counting the number of "Yes" responses and marking the total in the box provided. Once the self-evaluations have been completed, use the results to generate a discussion of the nine broad skill areas covered in the checklist, how each area is made up of different strategies, and how the *Study Strategies Made Easy* program is built on these strategies. Guide students to draw conclusions that developing good study strategies can help them improve their grades and reach their academic goals. Have students identify study strategies they presently use and discuss how they feel such strategies have helped them in the past. Students who discover their own needs are more likely to be proactive about making changes.

CHAPTER INTRODUCTIONS

Each of the chapters in the *Study Skills Made Easy* program covers a study skill area which is, in turn, divided into specific strategies. There is a brief introduction to each skill area explaining the importance of and purpose for learning the strategies that are included for that skill. Start each chapter by giving an overview of the skill and the strategies which will be covered. Be motivating and positive about how these strategies will help your students gain independence and improve their grades.

SUGGESTED PRESENTATION STRATEGIES

CHAPTER 1: ORGANIZATION

A good attention-grabber for this chapter is to ask a few of your good-natured students to volunteer to empty the entire contents of their book bags onto their desks. (It's fun to persuade the students whose bags you expect will be disasters!) Students will readily see the difference in organization among their classmates when the book bags are examined. Lead students in a discussion about the reasons for having well-organized notebooks and book bags. Point out that organization of materials is only one type of organization that is important. Successful people usually keep their work or study areas organized, their time managed, and their long-term projects planned out to have control over their busy lives.

Organizing Your School Supplies
Discuss each heading in the School Supplies Shopping List and direct students to check all materials they will need to buy. Lead a discussion about the importance of having proper school supplies. Ask students for examples of times when they were most inconvenienced because they ran out of a supply they needed for a project or assignment (e.g. going to a friend's house at midnight to borrow graph paper, etc.). Encourage students to use the School Supplies Shopping List when they go to the store to purchase needed supplies.

Organizing Your Study Area
A comfortable study environment with organized materials encourages positive study habits. Lead students in a discussion about where they presently do school work and keep their materials. Encourage students to suggest changes that could be made in their study environment. Students will list their suggestions at the bottom of the student page.

Organizing Your Time
Ask students if they usually have enough time to do school work and also participate in outside activities. Explain that in the business world, budgeting time is rated as a #1 necessity for success. Dozens of books and courses are offered to top executives who need to learn the skill of organization. If the leaders in business know that time management is a key to success, students need to know it, too. Let your students know how important it is to learn this strategy now.

Have students complete their Weekly Schedule Sheet found on page 8 for one week. Direct them to bring this completed sheet back to class to discuss and evaluate how they are spending their time. Then, ask students to complete the exercise "Evaluating How You Organized Your Time" on page 9. Encourage students to share changes they need to make that would allow them to handle their time more efficiently. On the next student page, students will find a second schedule sheet. Have them fill this out with the changes they decided would improve the efficiency of their time management. Remind students that this is only a guide, to be kept at home for reference.

Prioritizing Your Work

Define prioritizing as listing activities in their order of importance. Ask students how they decide which school work to do first. Some will say they do the work that needs to be turned in right away, others may do the hardest work first to get it out of the way, and still other students may prefer to do easy assignments first and harder ones next. The important idea about prioritizing is that students actively plan the order for doing their work.

Introduce the directions as students list their assignments for the day in any order. To complete this exercise, students may have to use assignments from a previous day. Students then consider their individual priorities and number each assignment accordingly. After students have kept their lists for several days, discuss their effectiveness and whether they need to make changes in how they prioritize their work loads. Advise students to either copy the *Get It Done Today* sheet in the appendix or buy a commercially prepared pad.

Organizing Your Grades

Ask students if they've ever been surprised by poor mid-semester interims or deficiencies or even report card grades. Follow directions with students using the sample Grade Chart as your guide. Encourage students to keep up their Grade Chart found on page 14. Try to check it during the quarter.

Organizing Your Long-Term Research Projects

Most students put off doing long-term research projects until the last minute. However, doing so can lead to rushed, inaccurate work that is far below what the student actually would be capable of doing had the project been better planned. Lead students to discuss how they plan out long-term projects, and how waiting until the last minute to do projects causes panic. Next, review the Goal -Setting Form for a Long-Term Research Project found on page 16. Go over each part of the form with the students using the following explanations.

REQUIREMENTS

Write the research project assignment from the sample form (page 16) on the board:
Research Paper: *"The Environment and Ways to Improve It"*

Review each item in the Requirement box in the sample, explaining that by writing all of the teacher's requirements, students will be sure not to leave anything out.

THE PRE-WRITE

Emphasize how important this phase of research is. Tell students that this phase should take approximately one-quarter of the entire research time. Present each step of the sample Goal-Setting Form. The following are additional suggestions for presenting some of the steps (others are self-explanatory):

STEP 2: All too often students choose a topic before researching whether there is enough information available. By that time it is too late to change topics and the quality of their work suffers. Therefore, make sure that students understand that following step 2 will save them time and help them get the best grade possible.

140

STEP 5: Once students choose a broad topic, they need to narrow it. They can do this by asking questions about their topics, such as "What is it about pollution that I want to explore?" We suggest that you list a few broad topics for students to narrow. Here are a few possibilities.

> Broad: Pollution
> Narrow: 1. Five methods to clean up pollution.
>   2. How teenagers can get involved in preventing and reducing pollution.
> Broad: Government of the U.S.
> Narrow: 1. Compare the three branches of the U.S. government.
>   2. Compare the responsibilities and powers of state and federal governments.
>   3. How do laws affect us in (your city)?

THE FIRST WRITE:

This phase should take approximately one-half of the total research time.

STEP 6:   If students don't know what brainstorming is, explain that all they need to do is let subtopics which relate to the topic freely flow through their minds, regardless of importance. They write all their ideas and then from that list, choose the three that will work best.

STEP 7:   Writing a thesis statement may be a new experience for some of your students. Therefore, you may want to spend a lesson teaching how to formulate a good thesis statement. The thesis statement usually comes at the end of the introductory first paragraph. Its purpose is to state the topic, your point of view or opinion about the topic, and the organization of your paper. Students can think of the thesis as a mini-outline of their entire paper.

> Examples of thesis statements:
>
> *1. In order to understand how the environment is being damaged (topic), one must study air (subtopic 1), water (subtopic 2), and noise (subtopic 3) pollution of the area.*
>
> *2. The most important technological advancement in the twentieth century has been the computer (topic) because it has affected business (subtopic 1), education (subtopic 2), and communication (subtopic 3) on a global basis.*
>
> *3. People should learn to play soccer (topic) because it teaches how to be part of a team (subtopic 1), improves physical fitness (subtopic 2), and is a major sport throughout the world (subtopic 3).*

STEP 9: Rough Outline

Show students how to turn one of the examples of thesis statements above (or one of your own) into a rough outline.

STEP 10: Note Cards

Explain that the purpose of both note cards and bibliography cards is to allow students to keep track of the facts they gather.

Points to emphasize:

1. Well-organized cards = well-organized research.

2. Paraphrasing prevents plagiarism.
3. One idea per note card means easier reference for writing.
4. Well-done note cards should be saved for possible future use (plastic index card files are helpful for storage)
5. Accurate and consistent coding is invaluable if students need to re-check information.
6. Sort cards to coincide with the outline and then write the paper by sticking to that order.

Sample Bibliography Card:

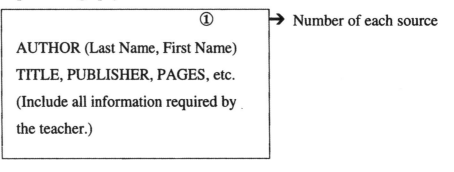

Number of each source

AUTHOR (Last Name, First Name)

TITLE, PUBLISHER, PAGES, etc.

(Include all information required by the teacher.)

Sample Note Card:

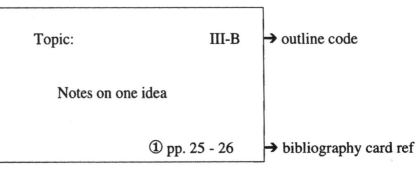

Topic: III-B → outline code

Notes on one idea

① pp. 25 - 26 → bibliography card ref

THE HOME STRETCH:
The last one quarter of the research time should be used to revise, rewrite, edit, and finalize.

CHAPTER 2: LEARNING STYLES

Before introducing this chapter, use the following attention-grabber that quickly lets students realize that each of us has a uniquely personal way of learning information. Tell students that they will have seven minutes to memorize these states and their capitals using any method and any materials at their desk that they wish.

1. Augusta, Maine
2. Concord, New Hampshire
3. Montpelier, Vermont
4. Providence, Rhode Island
5. Hartford, Connecticut
6. Albany, New York
7. Trenton, New Jersey
8. Harrisburg, Pennsylvania
9. Dover, Delaware
10. Annapolis, Maryland

When the seven minutes are up, tell students that they may not refer to any books or notes that they've used. Let them know that they won't be graded, but should do their best. Have students quickly write the ten states and capitals they have learned. After students are done, ask who correctly learned all ten, then nine, etc. Then, have students describe the specific methods they used to learn the information. You will generally find that students varied widely in the techniques they used to learn the states and their capitols. Continue the discussion by pointing out that each of us has our own way of learning and one way is not better than another if it works. Three strategies (Understanding How You Learn Best, What's Your Best Learning Environment?, and Your Personality and Your Learning Style) will allow students to understand that individual learning preferences, such as preferred time of day to study, where one studies, whether one studies better alone or with others, and whether someone remembers information best that is heard, seen, or acted upon all go into making up a person's learning style.

CHAPTER 3: COMMUNICATION STRATEGIES

Introduce this chapter by reviewing the introduction and discussing the importance of good communication skills. Have students relate positive and negative experiences they have had communicating with teachers and students. An important concept for students to derive from this chapter is that the way they communicate their thoughts and feelings through words, tone of voice, and non-verbal messages plays a major role in how effective their communication is.

Teacher Pleasing Behaviors

You may wish to add your own "pet peeves" to this list. Explain to students that if they have behaved in ways that "bug" teachers they can use this strategy to improve the opinion and attitude of those teachers toward them. After students fill out the strategy sheet, discuss each positive behavior with them as well as any additional ideas they may have.

Understanding Teachers' Expectations

Teachers are unique! (How's that for a novel concept to introduce to students?) Explain to students that by tailoring their work habits to teachers' unique methods of presentation, they will better meet their teachers' expectations, which will then increase their chances to earn good grades.

Communication with Teachers

Add your own situations for role playing with students. Some suggestions are:
1. Due to personal problems an assignment isn't done.
2. The teacher says you're missing an assignment, and you say you turned it in on time.
3. You are having difficulty completing homework because of the amount assigned, and you think it needs to be reduced.

You may wish to divide students into groups and let them present mini-plays about these situations. Many students need to learn practical ways to positively and effectively communicate with authority figures, so provide very specific feedback.

Cooperative Planning

This strategy is included for those students whose needs are not being met in daily classroom situations. This strategy is also designed to encourage students to independently identify problem areas and think about possible solutions. Students are then encouraged to become their own advocates and using good communication skills, approach a teacher for cooperative planning.

Discuss with students that they will need to decide if and when parents should be brought into this process.

Communicating with Other Students

Good communication skills are essential for making and keeping friends. Social skills research indicates that three skills (showing empathy, self-control, and cooperativeness), in particular, are very important. Lead students to define each of these skills and to discuss examples of empathy, self-control, and cooperativeness and how they affect relationships. Then have students complete the checklist on page 30 and continue the discussion.

Increasing Empathy Toward Others, Developing Self-Control, and Cooperativeness

These strategies are designed to help students communicate and develop in ways that improve relationships. These strategies and their exercises lend themselves to excellent dialogue and immediate application in school and at home.

CHAPTER 4: READING COMPREHENSION STRATEGIES

Before students can effectively use a textbook, they must be able to understand the content. In this chapter, the first two strategies are designed to give students practice in identifying the main ideas and supporting details of a reading selection, essential skills for reading comprehension. The remaining strategies included in this chapter reinforce the reading skills and focus upon effective usage of textbooks in content area classes.

Reading to Understand and Paraphrasing

These two strategies are the foundation for good reading comprehension and are the prerequisites to using the textbook effectively. Present the exercises in these two strategies using a three phase method: Modeling, Guided Practice and Independent Practice.

Exercise 1 — *modeling:* Modeling is actually doing the exercise for the students. As you read the passage aloud, you share your thoughts and reasons with students.

Exercise 2 — *guided practice*: Guided practice is meant for you to provide immediate feedback to students as they do the exercise. You may wish to use this as a group exercise that allows students to share their ideas.

Exercise 3 — *independent practice:* Independent practice is the point at which students work on their own. You may then meet with students to review their work and provide constructive feedback as to what is being done correctly and what areas may require practice.

Signal Words

Review each category of signal words and the examples for each. After your lesson, direct students to the exercise. Students can use pages from their own texts for additional practice. Remind students that they are circling signals now only to learn how they signal important content. After learning the strategy, they will not be required to circle signals.

Learning New Vocabulary

This strategy should be fun for students to practice. Encourage students to share their associations from the exercise or from any new words they are learning in their classes and to retain their vocabulary cards or notebooks for future reference tools.

3 SWEEPS of How to Really Read a Textbook

After your students master the 3 SWEEPS Strategy, provide practice using students' own social studies and science textbooks. We suggest that you initially check students' highlighting, since they usually begin by highlighting too much. After they practice this strategy to read school texts, you may want to allow students to check each others' work. In schools or centers where students cannot highlight in their textbooks, teach Note-Taking Strategies next, with particular emphasis on Adding Textbook Notes to Lecture Notes. While this strategy takes time to master, its effectiveness is long-term, and perfect for students planning to attend college.

CHAPTER 5: NOTE-TAKING STRATEGIES

Note-taking is obviously a very important skill for your students to learn. In this section we have included strategies for outlining, mind mapping, and taking combo notes. The students will also become familiar with common abbreviations used in note-taking and how to turn their notes into study sheets by using recall questions. Separate strategies for taking notes from textbooks and from lectures are also included. When introducing students to note-taking, follow the modeling, guided and independent practice teaching strategies described above in chapter 4.

Students usually take notes in class during discussions or lectures, but they often don't realize that there may be more than one method of taking notes. And they often don't use their notes to help them study from their textbooks and outside readings. These strategies will teach them how to make their notes work for them. Emphasize that note-taking can be a powerful tool for successful learning if notes are organized, accurate, and legible.

Simple Outlining - Mind-Mapping - Combo Notes

Three methods for note-taking are presented. Students may not choose to use all three methods to take notes. However, teach all three, explaining that students will be able to choose different organizations for different situations. Use the samples in each of these note-taking strategies as your guide to present the directions for each method.

Notice that for each strategy (Simple Outlining, Mind-Mapping, Combo Notes), we have included an exercise for students to read a selection and take notes on it. In their books they have skeletal outlines to fill in with the headings to help them. Observe that students are including the correct details for each exercise. There are additional reading selections in Appendix D for extra practice. We also suggest that you have students independently take notes from their textbooks and that they then check their accuracy.

SIMPLE OUTLINING - Most of your students have probably learned how to outline. The focus of this lesson is not the outline itself, but how to choose the information to include and then how to organize it.

MIND-MAPPING - The lessons for mind-mapping include Mind-Mapping Madness that provide examples of various formats to organize specific types of information. These are only guides. Provide additional examples of text and have students create their own mind maps. This can be done as an individual or small group exercise. More artistic students can be encouraged to create more picture-like mind maps.

COMBO NOTES - The Combo Note strategy does exactly what the title implies—it combines the organization of an outline with the creative freedom of a mind map. This method is sometimes less intimidating and more practical to many students.

Using Abbreviations

Discuss the importance of using abbreviations as a short-cut for in note-taking. Allow students to share any abbreviations that they use in their notes.

Using Recall Questions to Turn Your Notes into Super Study Sheets

Recall questions are valuable study aids and have proven to be one of the strategies most appreciated and utilized by students. By preparing recall questions, students can easily review notes for class and study for exams. This strategy reviews the importance of recall questions and how to use them when taking notes from lectures. We suggest you plan to model this strategy and provide guided practice. Students can write recall questions for the additional readings in Appendix D.

Emphasize to students these results of many scientific studies:
1. People who review notes within 24 hours of taking notes retain about 80% of the information. People who wait to review retain only 40%.
2. People who review material periodically can recall up to 100%. People who don't frequently review retain only up to 40%.

Remind your students that 100% recall equals an "A" grade, while 40% equals an "F." This strategy can make that much of a difference on any test, but for mid-terms and finals it is vital.

Students should write recall questions for all the note-taking exercises they did in *Study Strategies Made Easy*. Then, for independent practice, students should write recall questions from their own science and/or social studies textbooks. Point out to students that if they are not required to take notes from their textbooks, they have the option to write recall questions directly from information they highlighted in their textbooks. They can number the information in their texts and write the recall questions using the same numbers on notebook paper. Periodically invite students to show you their recall questions for feedback.

Remind students that recall questions will work well only if they review them consistently. If students think you are adding to their homework time, explain that reviewing one page of recall questions should take only a few minutes and save hours of time needed to relearn forgotten material. Also, ask if a few minutes of review for an "A" grade is worth their time.

Improving Your Listening Power

In both high school and college about 80% of a student's time is spent listening to instructors. Outside school, the percentage of time we spend listening is at least as high. Therefore, it pays to "improve your listening power." This strategy teaches students the importance of verbal cues, presentation cues, and body language cues when listening to someone talk. Lead a discussion about the different cues given by people during conversation. After students complete the two observation exercises, discuss the different cues used by newscasters and teachers.

Taking Notes from Lectures

This strategy provides valuable troubleshooting tips for the student having difficulty taking notes. You may want to use any of the selections in this book as a lecture rather than an assigned reading exercise for practice of this strategy. Or, use your usual class lesson to provide practice.

Adding Textbook Notes to Lecture Notes

Lectures do not always include all the details that students are expected to know. Therefore, students need to learn efficient ways to identify and combine information from texts with their lecture notes. Students will know for which teachers this is important by referring to "Understanding Teachers' Expectations."

CHAPTER 6: MEMORIZATION STRATEGIES

Using the introductory page, instruct students about how our memories work. They can choose techniques to use depending upon the type of information to be learned, the length of time it will need to be retained, and their own unique learning styles.

Remembering Requires Understanding and Planning

Use this strategy to help students discover that :
1. understanding aids memorization
2. there is a great amount of information given to them, so they must be selective in choosing what to memorize
3. they must choose those memory techniques that work best for their particular style of learning. Encourage students to refer to the memory technique chart on page 72 to match technique to styles. However, remind students to try all techniques before eliminating any.

Ten Memory Techniques

Introduce students to ten different ways to memorize information. Review the learning styles chart on page 72, reminding students to choose the memory techniques that match their learning style. We suggest you teach 1 to 3 of the memory strategies per lesson and give students time to practice. Use the follow-up exercise when you are finished teaching all the strategies listed below.

Memorizing by Using Acrostics and Acronyms

Memorizing by Using Charting and Visual Emphasis

Memorizing by Using Visualization

Memorizing by Using Association

Memorizing by Linking Information

Memorizing by Using Rehearsal

Suggested Follow-Up Exercise:

Students will use their science or social studies textbooks and notes. Assign students to choose two or three memorization techniques they will use for their next test. They will list the type of information and the techniques they will use and bring it in for you to provide feedback.

CHAPTER 7: TEST-TAKING STRATEGIES

Use the "Study Habits Checklist" on page 83 as the attention-grabber for this strategy. Discuss with students whether their grades are reflecting their efforts.

Tell students that they will now take a test. All materials should be off desks except for *Study Strategies Made Easy* and a pencil. They will have five minutes to complete the test. Tell students to remain quiet during and upon completion of the test. Students should now turn to page 81. At the end of five minutes, make sure that all students got the point—always read all directions before you begin a test.

Taking Objective Tests and Taking Subjective Tests

Present each type of test. Do and check all exercises. Relate these to the tests students are actually taking in their content classes. Note: The test on page 92 is a cumulative test of all objective test strategies. Students should relearn any area that they could not recall.

Making Old Tests Work for You

Our plea to teachers: We are aware of the problems you have returning tests to students. However, please, please try to return the questions and a student's answers if at all possible. If not, allow ample time for review. Encourage students to use this strategy for a truly effective review and plan for improving test grades.

Studying for Mid-Terms and Final Exams

This strategy is relevant regardless at what point of the school year you are teaching it. Students should be using the strategies in *Study Strategies Made Easy* consistently enough that studying for mid-terms or finals is a breeze!

CHAPTER 8: HANDLING HOMEWORK

The purpose of this chapter is to acknowledge students' discomfort (and real displeasure) with homework and to offer them strategies to ease the "burden." Lead a discussion about what students think about homework, e.g., Is homework necessary?, When don't you mind homework assignments?, What is the purpose for teachers giving homework?

Homework – Ugh!
This strategy is intended to get students to balance the negative aspects of having homework with the positive ones.

Homework Habits Checklist
Ask students to complete the Homework Habits Checklist on page 104. This is designed to help students understand their preparation for doing homework, their attitude towards assignments, and the time they allot for homework in their schedule. It ends by asking students what changes they might make to improve their homework habits.

Homework Hassles, Homework Helpers
Discuss the tips in this strategy with students to encourage good homework habits.

Doing Homework Pays Dividends
Students will answer the questions in this strategy and discuss their answers as a group.

CHAPTER 9: STRESS MANAGEMENT STRATEGIES

Students feel stress for a myriad of reasons, most of which we as teachers can neither address nor relieve. Educators acutely understand that stress and/or negative feelings greatly decrease students' achievement. Therefore, this chapter's strategies provide students with ways to alleviate some of the stress they may feel and improve their chances for academic success.

Staying Relaxed under Stress
On the board write: STUDY STRATEGIES MADE EASY. Tell students to use the letters in those words to form as many words as possible in five minutes. Tell them a prize will be awarded, so they should not show their list. After each minute, let students know how much time is remaining. After the five minutes are up, ask students the following questions:
1. How many of you think you won?
2. How many think you didn't win?
3. How many felt stress to complete this quickly or with enough words to win?

Now ask about the symptoms of stress they felt such as stomach in knots, heart racing, hands perspiring, mind going blank, etc. These would be negative and not very helpful. Refer students to page 110 and have them check off their stress indicators. You may also want to mention that stress that can be handled can be okay to feel when faced with new or difficult or important situations.

Using Visualization to Relax

Lead students in a discussion about the different ways they have found to relax. Introduce the concept of "visualization" and discuss how visualizing ourselves in a relaxed setting and thinking of positive, relaxing thoughts can help promote physical and mental relaxation. First, model how you would do a relaxation strategy. (A day at the beach or in the mountains?) Lead the students in the visualization exercise in class as they try to relax as a group. Afterward, discuss their reactions and what they experienced both mentally and physically during this process.

Handling Test Anxiety

Almost every student has had the experience of feeling nervous or tense before a test. Sometimes, this tension can reach a level which is so high that it can affect a student's concentration and performance. When this happens frequently before tests, the student may suffer from test anxiety. Discuss with students the possible causes of test anxiety and review some of the ways they can reduce nervousness before a test. Then go through the exercise on page 113 to show students how they can reduce anxiety by repeatedly thinking of stressful situations and relaxing.

Reaching Goals through Affirmations

Before reviewing "Reaching Goals through Affirmations" use the following exercise. Before class, have four blank papers taped on the walls just above the reach of your students. Choose four students, give each a marker or crayon, and have each stand in front of one of the papers. Tell them to reach as high as they think they can and draw a horizontal line. Now, tell students that they reached high but that you have confidence that they can reach even higher. Give a lot of positive encouragement. Tell students to try again. You should see lines higher this time. Be very positive and let students know that it was their new self-confidence and increased effort that allowed them to stretch to reach beyond their initial expectations. That is exactly what they can apply to the goals they set for themselves in all areas of their lives.

Now that they see how positive "self-talk" helps to reach goals, they can complete the strategy.

Now That We Have Finished . . .A Self-Evaluation Post-Test

Have students complete The Checklist of Study Strategies on page 115 to see how they score after having finished the *Study Strategies Made Easy* program. After students complete the evaluation and score it, compare their scores to the ones received the first time they completed the checklist in the Before We Begin section. Discuss the changes that they made in the course of the program. Students will then complete the exercise. Guide students to verbalize the fact that they now can be more in control of how they perform in school, that they can broaden their choices, and contiinue to increase their accomplishments.

Be sure to remove the certificate from students' books and fill it out for each participant.

Congratulations!

Appendix D
Additional Exercises
for Note-Taking

Acid Rain

The term "acid rain" is actually redundant since rain is naturally acidic, measuring 6 on the PH scale, with 7 being neutral. Rain reacts with elements in the air, namely carbon dioxide and sulfur dioxide, forming a weak acid. However, there are other elements in the air that react to make rain even more acidic than it is. Fumes from burning oil and coal are two elements that contribute to the higher acidity of rain, and can bring the pH up between 3 and 5.5. In this way, the acidic rain can damage plant and animal life. In fact, natural rain can dissolve limestone and form caves, but acid rain can damage the much harder stone used to make buildings and statues, and even make them unrecognizable.

Archimedes

"Eureka!" is actually a Greek word meaning "I've found it!" This famous phrase was uttered 2,000 years ago by a Greek philosopher named Archimedes while running home, undressed, from a bath. Archimedes was asked by the king to find out whether his new crown was made of pure gold or if it had silver added to it. If the crown had silver, it would be lighter than if it were made with all gold. Archimedes wondered how he could measure this. One day, when stepping into his bathtub, he noticed that he caused the water to flow over the edge. It made him realize that the amount of water the crown would displace would equal the volume of the crown itself. All he had to do was compare the volume of the crown to a chunk of gold that was the same weight as the crown, and thus, the king would have his answer. Archimedes was so excited by his discovery that he ran from the tub shouting "Eureka!" all the way home.

Fireworks

One common aspect of almost all Fourth of July celebrations is the fireworks display. Even in states where it is illegal for citizens to set off fireworks, pyrotechnics experts are able to put on awesome displays for everyone's entertainment. Fireworks are dangerous because of the combinations of chemicals that are used. These chemicals must be handled with care, and this is what pyrotechnics experts are able to do. Fireworks themselves are cardboard tubes filled with gunpowder. When heated, oxygen inside the rocket is released and this encourages the burn. The colors that are displayed are actually different chemicals. Strontium produces red fireworks, barium produces green, and sodium produces yellow. So, at the next Fourth of July celebration, you'll be able to appreciate the fireworks and know the chemicals that make people "ooh" and "ahh."

Ice

Everyone has encountered ice in their lives (some more than others, depending on where you live), but have you really thought about what ice is? When most liquids freeze, the solid form of their liquid sinks. However, when water freezes, its solid form, ice, floats. The reason for this is that water expands when it freezes, so ice is actually lighter than water. Water freezes at 32 degrees Fahrenheit, but if you add an impurity, such as salt, the freezing point lowers. When this happens, it needs to be colder in order for the water to freeze. This is why people put salt on roads and walkways in places where it snows during the winter. Another interesting point involves ice skaters. Ice melts under pressure, so the pressure of ice skaters' skates causes the ice to melt, and therefore, the ice skaters are actually gliding on water!

Volcanoes

Locations

Volcanoes are not located everywhere on the earth. In fact, they can exist only in very specific places. Almost all volcanoes are found at or near the edges of tectonic plates. The cracks in the plates allow melted rock to rise up to the surface and form volcanoes. Many volcanoes are found along the edges of the Pacific Plate in Japan, Alaska, Central America, South America, and Indonesia. This location forms a circle on the global map, and is therefore called the "Ring of Fire."

Composition

There are two common features that all volcanoes have below the surface: magma and the chimney. A chimney, or pipe, is the passageway that carries magma to the earth's surface. These chimneys may be just a few miles below the surface, but some chimneys are hundreds of miles deep. The magma which they carry is a pool of melted rock and gas that pushes toward the surface. As the magma rises, gases are released which may cause an explosion that expels lava. Lava can be more than 2,100 degrees Fahrenheit, and the hotter the lava, the more yellow it appears. After lava hardens, it is known as basalt.

Mauna Loa

Hawaii has several volcanoes on its many islands. The tallest of the three active volcanoes found on the Big Island of Hawaii is Mauna Loa. The ocean around Hawaii is tens of thousands of feet deep, and the islands themselves are formed from tons of lava piling up to protrude from the ocean. Mauna Loa's base is 70 miles wide, and its total height, above and below water, is almost six miles. This means that it is taller than Mount Everest, and, unlike mountains, active volcanoes can grow taller over many years.

Birdbrains

Sometimes when we want to tease a person, we use names of animals to do our dirty work. Some that come to mind are "sly as a fox," "dumb ox," or "lazy as a mule." The term "birdbrain" is often used to imply that someone is clueless, or unaware of what is around them. Wait just a minute. There are, after all, some really smart birds. Therefore, isn't this epithet unfair to the bird population? As it turns out, this may not be unfair in all cases. Since there are birds that do seem dumb enough to be "birdbrains." The woodpecker is only one example of a bird that does justice to the term "birdbrain." For instance, sometimes the woodpecker pecks a hole into a tree so fervently that it actually bores a hole right through to the other side. Even when this happens, the woodpecker, saving up for winter, continues to store nuts and seeds in the hole. He apparently fails to notice that the food is falling right out the other side of the tree. These poor, but truly birdbrain birds end up starving during the winter months. Thus, the woodpecker proves itself to be a true "birdbrain."

Another "birdbrain" is the turkey. One illustration is that when turkeys are young, they have to be taught to eat, lest they starve to death. Some turkey breeders have even been known to scatter feed on the floor right under the turkey's feet in hopes that they will get the message. Unfortunately, this is to no avail because the turkeys never take the hint, nor do they take the feed. Another sure sign that the turkey may be a true birdbrain comes when there is a rainstorm. Turkeys have been known to stare up into the rain with their beaks open, and before they get the hint to shut their mouths, they drown.

So, the next time you hear the term "birdbrain," think of these examples and decide if the term really suits the situation. The person you are teasing may be much too smart to be compared to these truly "birdbrain" birds.

Athletes Compete

It is fun to watch the athletes in the Olympics. They are considered the best athletes in their countries and their feats seem amazing. In the 1968 Olympics, in Mexico City, Robert Beamon broke world records in his long jump. Experts said that his record might never be broken because a longer jump could break bones or shred muscles. However, humans cannot compare to animals when it comes to athletic feats.

While they cannot do a lot of things that humans can do, animals seem to break our athletic records all the time. For instance, the tiny flea, in one jump, can go six inches into the air and two feet in length. In human lengths, that would mean a man jumping a quarter of a mile. Even Mr. Beamon might not be able to match that. And then there is the case of whales. Whales can dive 3,700 feet below the sea, yet even with special diving equipment, man has only gone down to 2,300 feet. The next impressive animal athlete is the penguin. Penguins move through water at 22 miles per hour, while humans have only been known to go 5.3 mph. Then, another human athlete, the skydiver, who jumps out of planes for quite a while before opening a parachute, can reach 185 miles per hour in a free fall. However, peregrine falcons can easily reach 225 mph without ever considering the use of a parachute. Finally, take the greyhound. No human yet can outrun his 40 miles per hour speed.

So, if the Olympic committee ever decides to let an animal athlete compete against a human athlete, the gold medal would be a very far reach for the human to win — maybe a little too far.

Do You Know about Matthew Alexander Henson?

"Stars and Stripes nailed to the North Pole — Peary." That was the message sent through the wire services about the first expedition to reach the North Pole. For centuries, men had attempted to get to the pole, but, while many died, none had succeeded. Then, on September 6, 1909, Admiral Robert Peary, an experienced adventurer, became the first man to reach the North Pole and live to report it. Or was he?

For years, the family of Peary's personal attendant, Matthew Henson, claimed that it was Henson, not Peary who had first stepped foot on the site. In the 1990s, historians came to agree that it well may have been Henson who should be credited with the feat. But who was Matthew Henson?

Matthew Alexander Henson was an African-American, born in 1866 in Maryland. He was orphaned early in his childhood, and by age twelve, set sail as a cabin boy on a ship. Upon his return he took a job as a store clerk in Washington D.C., where he met Robert Peary. Peary hired Henson to survey canals in Nicaragua, South America. From that time until Peary's death, the two men were associates in many adventures, concluding with the dangerous expedition to the North Pole.

In 1908, Peary set out to explore the Pole. Peary hired four Inuit, Alaskan Indians or Eskimos, who were invaluable guides and knew the torturous weather of the area. Henson was Peary's aide and handled the equipment and the all-important dog sleds. Finally, they reached the Pole and historians say that because it was Henson who planted the American Flag, he probably did take the first steps on the Pole. Henson wrote a book about his adventures called *A Negro Explorer at the North Pole*. He died in New York City on March 9, 1955.

It actually doesn't seem to matter which of the men took the first steps. What does matter is that these men were brave, worked well together for much of their lives, and made their mark on history.

How to Avoid Bad Luck
(At Least According to Superstition)

Superstition, according to *Webster's New World Dictionary*, is any belief or attitude based on fear or ignorance, that is inconsistent with the known laws of science or with what is generally considered in the particular society as true or rational, especially belief in charms, omens, or the supernatural. O.K., now that you know that superstition is based upon ignorance of facts, you would think that few people would be superstitious. You would be wrong. You might also be surprised by how many people believe superstitions— even some people that you know.

The truth is that many of us believe in some superstitions, even when we know it is silly. Here are some superstitions. See how many you know and how many you have been careful not to cross: Don't open an umbrella in the house. If you spill salt, throw more salt over your left (not your right) shoulder. Don't break a mirror if you don't want to be plagued by bad luck for seven years. If you say something that you wish wouldn't happen, quickly knock on wood or it will. On the other hand, if you say something that you are very thankful for, knock on that wood even more quickly or it could be taken away at any minute!! Wow, there are a lot of ways to incur bad luck if you believe in superstitions.

There are even superstitions as to how to get good luck. One is planting basil in front of your garden when you move into a new house. Another one is that if you want to get married, catch the bride's bouquet after the wedding. Try not to grab it before she walks down the aisle or you will most likely have immediate bad luck. One more way to catch good luck is to find a four leaf clover, preferably while working in the rain because that's said to guarantee really good luck (and maybe a cold).

The truth is, there is no proof at all that any of these superstitions will be the cause of either bad or good luck. In fact, seriously superstitious people sometimes bring their own troubles because they let superstitions rule their actions and therefore limit themselves. So, if you have fun knowing superstitions (and there are many more from every culture), that's fine. However, it is probably a good idea to remember that you can take charge of your own life and bring your own good luck. Also, it is better to believe in ideas that are sensible and bring you a true sense of happiness. Good luck!

Pranks, Jokes, and Hoaxes

People enjoy a good joke. Many jokes, though, are devised to trick someone. So, whether you think a joke is funny depends upon whether you are the joker or the jokee. Here are a few practical jokes that people have played. See if you would have been fooled.

Barrels of Fun

In the 1700s, during the American Revolution, an American general, Israel Putnam, invited a British general to test each man's nerves. The test was to see how long each of them would sit upon a barrel filled with gunpowder. After the fuses of each barrel were lit, the British general could sit no longer and fled. The American general and his troops loved the joke because only they knew that the barrels had been filled with onions.

The War of the Worlds

Many Americans were fooled in 1939 by a radio program called "The War of the Worlds." It was a terrible time in our country and in the world. There was a depression and people were afraid that we would be forced to enter World War II. Americans' moods were grim. On the radio (there was no television yet) came a horrified announcement that aliens had invaded Earth, landed in New Jersey, and were going to begin killing Earthlings. People who heard the report and didn't "get" the joke fled in panic. Finally, it was announced that it was all a hoax. Do you think the joke was funny? The bosses at the radio didn't. They fired the prankster, Orson Welles, who then went on to become a famous actor and director.

Pasta Prank

Another hoax occurred on April Fools' Day in 1957. A television program was aired showing a group of Italian women harvesting spaghetti. There were pictures of the women picking spaghetti from trees. Many viewers wrote to ask if they could attend the harvest and buy the freshly picked spaghetti. First, did you notice that the date of the report was April Fools' Day? That may have tipped you off that this was a joke. Do you get the joke? Spaghetti does not grow on trees.

A Hoax that Didn't Hatch

Finally, in Miami Florida, a professor called a news conference to announce that he would reveal the hatching of the extinct rock egg. A thousand people crowded into the park where the event was held. News reporters were there with their cameras. Out came the professor with a huge rock "egg." He went on and on for hours describing how significant this happening was, to witness an extinct egg. Eventually, people drifted away, getting bored when no rock egg hatched. The next day, the newspapers reported that the egg had hatched after everyone had left. This would have been very strange had it been true because as you know, if a species is extinct, it does not live anymore and a rock has no life within it anyway. Many Miamians were red-faced the next day, and it wasn't due to the hot Florida Sun.

CERTIFICATE OF ACHIEVEMENT

This certificate is presented to

for completion of *Study Strategies Made Easy*.

Our sincere congratulations are extended to you.

Leslie Davis

Leslie Davis, M.Ed

Sandi Sirotowitz

Sandi Sirotowitz, M.Ed.

Teacher

Date